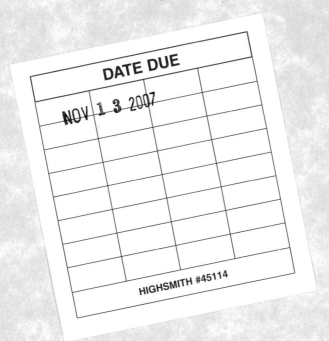

DATE DUE			
NOV 1 3 2007			
HIGHSMITH #45114			

Hitting Home

HITTING HOME

FEMINIST ETHICS, WOMEN'S WORK, AND THE BETRAYAL OF "FAMILY VALUES"

Gloria H. Albrecht

Continuum
New York London

2002

The Continuum International Publishing Group Inc
370 Lexington Avenue, New York, NY 10017

The Continuum International Publishing Group Ltd
The Tower Building, 11 York Road, London SE1 7NX

Printed in the United States of America

Library of Congress Cataloging-in-Publication Data

Albrecht, Gloria H.
    Hitting home : feminist ethics, women's work, and the betrayal
of "family values" / Gloria H. Albrecht.
        p. cm.
    Includes bibliographical references and index.
    ISBN 0-8264-1442-7 (hardcover)
    1. Women—United States—Economic conditions. 2. Work and
family—United States. 3. Family policy—United States. 4.
Capitalism—United States. 5. Feminist economics—United States. 6.
Social values—United States. 7. Social justice—United States. I.
Title.
HQ1381 .A44 2002
305.42'0973—dc21
                                                    2002010111

Contents

Preface

Before asking the reader to enter into a text that may prove heavy-going at times, and into data that can be overwhelming, it is more than appropriate to provide an overview. This is a work that combines social theory with social research, aggregate descriptions with individual portraits, and all for the purpose of developing a feminist ethical response to work and family issues. What follows is a brief sketch of overarching themes. (It is my hope that it will also serve as an enticement to read further.)

Two new contexts raise profound questions about the capacity of the present economic system to support human community. One, most ably described by Larry Rasmussen in *Earth Community Earth Ethics*, sets before us the constraints that exist because nature is a constellation of integrated systems of which we are also a part. Religious thinking, as well as economic beliefs and practices, that denies the interlocking oneness of our present existence and future survival leads us on a path of self-destruction that will be marked by crises of faith in the face of extreme suffering and violent confrontations. Rasmussen calls upon us, and upon religious traditions, "to be transformed, in the Spirit, *by* their crises."[1]

The second context exists within the first, of course, as does all life. More than two hundred years ago a momentum was unleashed in Europe and the United States by new economic arrangements. These arrangements cooperated with existing cultural practices to give elite white men the power to dominate the course of social change that was transforming both public and private spaces. In addition to the "apartheid thinking" by which modern Western thought divided humans from nature and human economies from natural ones, the economy of modernity was based on a division between the social activities related to the production of profit-earning goods and services and the social activities related to nurturance and caregiving. Ideologically, if not always in reality, two genders, two spaces, and two types of character were created to maintain that separation. Within the United States the meanings and purposes of productive work, gender identities and roles, family forms and practices, and social relationships of race and class were reformulated. The result was a social structure in which the activities of families and the activities of market-oriented work, while typically described as separate and distinct, functioned together in an uneasy interdependence.

The reconstruction of gender and family forms was key to this successful social transition. Shifts in gender roles and identities, in family size, and family strategies were necessary to implement and justify the new relationships. The Victorian, white, middle- and upper-income family ideal, created in the first half of the nineteenth century, existed, and exists today, with limited relevance to the actual lives of most women, men, and families and their experiences of domestic activities and market-oriented work. Yet, this ideal continues to impact political and judicial policies that define the family and design social legislation, economic practices reflected in corporate policies, and religious and cultural symbols prescribing values and morality. This discrepancy between the social ideal and the actual practices of many people reflects the encoding of social privilege into social rules. Privileged norms, that is, the norms of the privileged, were and are used to explain and justify disparities of well-being among races, classes, and genders.

Today, as the twenty-first century gets underway, a new momentum has been unleashed by revised economic practices. Most women and most mothers in the United States participate in the formal labor market while continuing to perform most of the unpaid family labor. This breach of the Victorian ideal is symptomatic of a new period of economic transformation. Beginning in the last half of the twentieth century, in the context of a global market, a complex of new economic arrangements has developed. In the United States, these practices involve a shift away from industrial capitalism and a shift toward employment in the service and information-technology sectors. As always, new economic arrangements include, and depend on, cooperative public policies. Today this political economy, known as neoliberalism, requires the re-forming of what are assumed to be "noneconomic" social patterns: gender identities and roles, family forms and practices, and the social relationships of race and class.

A primary source of the "family crisis"—so prevalent in public discourse—is the instability and conflict created as people and families respond to new economic and social conditions. Families *are* being battered by the constant expansion of economic rationality into their lives and by the need to radically reorganize family life in response to the demands of the workplace. However, the dominant response of public intellectuals, government figures, and many ethicists has been to encode as new social norms the strategies of the socially advantaged. Once again privileged norms are used to explain and justify the ongoing and widening disparities of well-being among races, classes, and genders.

My intent is to look at these economic changes and this sense of family crisis through a particular lens—that of women's experiences with work. My judgments arise out of moral commitments that are not all that unique: a commitment to women's social equality and a commitment to what has traditionally been women's work—the well-being of families. My arguments arise out of a careful look at "what is." What *is* the actual material reality of women's work experiences? Consequently, some of the chapters in this book are heavily laden with data. The proliferation of statistics, concrete examples, and individual voices from specific lives may seem excessive to some readers. The large amount of data may become tedious. I hope not. The statistical data are essential. They dissect the aggregate data often presented in order to disclose what *women* are actually experiencing. They provide a grounding in women's reality for the views I am presenting. In particular these data serve to expose most current talk about family values as, at its best, ethereal and baseless; at its worse, it is profoundly elitist, comfortable with social privilege and the inequality privilege sustains. Extensive endnotes amplify the data, provide specific examples, clarify how data are interpreted and their limits, and provide additional sources for further contributions to this discussion. Since this additional information deepens my argument, I have placed these notes at the end of each chapter to make them more accessible to the reader. Without grounding ethical arguments in such specificity, social ethics runs the risk of not dealing with the reality of most people's lives and of not seeing the actual (and differing) impacts on women's lives of public policies and economic decisions that appear justified from other, often more abstract, perspectives.

I begin in chapter 1 by describing significant aspects of the contemporary context of work, my methods of social analysis, and the commitments that guide my analysis. Chapter 2 is a brief history of women's relationship to *work*. The social conflict that constructed the contemporary understanding of this word becomes clear as this history documents the relationship that exists between changing economic practices and the revision of social norms and values. In chapters 3 and 4, I describe the material realities of women as they take, or are assigned, responsibility in this new economy for both producing income and reproducing social life. Chapter 3 investigates the issue of caregiving that arises in response to most women's participation in the labor force; chapter 4 describes the rising conflict over time as neoliberalism intensifies capitalism's insistence that time is money.

Having looked through the lens of women's work—that place where productive work and the work of social reproduction merge—I argue in chapter 5 that commitment to women's equality and to families' well-being is the second challenge that, along with environment concerns, re-opens an ethical critique of the nature of capitalism itself. The values found within Christian economic ethics, when responsive to women's equality and to families' well-being, will guide that critique.

It is probably clear by now that when I place "what is" against "what ought to be," I find a disparity that calls for impassioned resistance and change on behalf of women, children, the poor, and, ultimately, the earth itself. Such pockets of passion do exist despite the economic rationality (cost/benefit analysis) penetrating human community. They exist in every part of the globe. They exist in the many social sciences on which a social ethicist must rely. My many footnotes will reveal the impassioned researchers to whom I am so indebted. Pockets of passion also exist in Baltimore, where I spent about ten years in urban ministry. They exist here in Detroit despite, maybe because of, Detroit's experience of dramatic economic loss and hostile abandonment.[2] I am grateful to such people and their prophetic work. Few of us can maintain a sense of sanity and continue our work of resistance alone. I admire the prophets who can do this, but I am not one of them. Therefore, I especially want to thank my colleagues and friends in Baltimore and here in Detroit who have the courage to live without innocence and to endure the moral discomfort that comes from seeing one's own privileges in connection with others' deprivation; who have the capacity for outrage and the courage to show it; and, finally, who have the virtue of submission to a passion that energizes their work for justice. Of many, I especially mention Stephanie Mitchem, Jane Schaberg, and Margaret and Leonard Weber. Most of all I thank my partner-in-life, Tom Schindler, for sharing with me his life and his passion for justice.

NOTES

1. Larry Rasmussen, *Earth Community Earth Ethics* (Maryknoll, N.Y.: Orbis Books, 1996), 14.

2. Stephanie Mitchem has brought to my attention a report to the Archdiocese of Detroit that found a 193 percent increase in poverty in Detroit between 1980 and 1990, with 40 percent of the population living in poverty. See Myron Orfield, *Detroit Metropolitics: A Regional Agenda for Community and Stability* (Report to the Archdiocese of Detroit: 1999), 5.

1

Framing the Issue: Contexts, Methods, and Commitments

. . . at this moment we are confronted by this alternative: either the emerging global village will be fashioned into a radical democratic confederation that is governed by interests in favor of the economic well-being and political rights of all its citizens without exception, or this global situation will become subject to a tightly controlled, "soft-gloved" dictatorship that concentrates all economic and cultural resources in the hands of a few and relegates the majority to a permanent impoverished and dehumanized underclass.[1]

EVERY AGE SEEMS TEMPTED to see itself at a turning point critical to the shape of the future. Sometimes this sense of grand drama is a product of hubris rooted in the experience of power. Sometimes it is a product of deep moral concern. Our age, this age of fracturing and reconstituting family forms amidst complex global interactions, welcomed and resisted, is different from others only in terms of those specific changes that give rise to pride in some and fear in others. The future will tell which was better founded.

My purpose here is to enter the current discussion about the future of modern society and, particularly, the future of women and their families. The discussion is, at its base, a struggle over conflicting views of what constitutes a good society and what sustains it. Yet, this discussion often takes place at a high level of abstraction. Too little attention is given to the real contexts of ordinary people—of women, mothers, and children, especially. So my intent is to inquire into the daily lives of women and their experiences of work—both unpaid and income-producing work—as their experiences have been shaped by economic changes that began in the United States halfway through the twentieth century. In particular, these economic changes have reshaped the lives of middle- and upper-income white women, their families, and their relationship to work for wages. Consequently, they have also reshaped these women's relationships to the well-being of other, economically poorer, women.

Some of these changes are celebrated as real advances in "the longest revolution" of women's struggle for access to the full range of human and citizenship rights. I, however, am suspicious. Other changes, especially changes in family forms, are too often targeted as the root of most social ills. My suspicion deepens. How good do these changes appear if the ethical criteria we apply include the equality of women and the well-being of families?

The answer I give to that question differs from that of some others because of where I choose to stand in making a response. For example, feminism separates my views from social conservatives such as William Bennett. But my stance in a Christian liberatory tradition also distances my views from conservative Christian ethicists, such as Max Stackhouse, and from self-described liberals in the family-crisis debate, such as Don Browning, as well as from economic liberals, such as Lisa Sowle Cahill, with whom I am more likely to share some practical strategies. To provide a rationale and a roadmap to what follows, I offer here in summary fashion the presuppositions I bring to this dialogue: my reading of the global context in which we now live and the impact that context has on the lives of women and families. I also set out the methodology that I use as well as the fundamental commitments that have led me to choose this method and these materials.

CONTEXTS

Contemporary Economic Contexts

Globalization
Globalization is differently defined depending on how one makes the distinction between continuity and change. At its most obvious, globalization simply refers to the reality of an expanded, now worldwide, marketplace. This exchange of goods and services connects the lives of people living at

great geographic and cultural distances from one another. That, of course, is a centuries-old phenomenon, a *continuity*.

But, globalization also refers to the geographic extension of existing economic practices with two important differences: (1) these market exchanges can take place with tremendous speed; and (2) these exchanges now include not just product markets but huge financial and labor markets as well. Lying behind these changes in a world of very uneven economic conditions among countries, and among groups within countries, is a singular, Western, and North Atlantic economic theory and practice that has come to dominate the promotion of this highly interconnected system of world trade.

This economic form, called neoliberalism, is not simply the natural extension of global trade, nor even of capitalism. It is a political economic theory within capitalism that places great faith in the ability of unregulated markets to find the best economic balance among multiple players and the best solutions to an increasing number of social problems. Neoliberal globalization calls for national policies that emphasize export production, privatization and deregulation, reductions in government-sector employment and expenditures (especially reductions in social services), and fiscal policies that promote the international movement of capital, credit incentives for producers, and reductions in business taxes and tariffs. These policies are explained and defended by appeals to freedom. A free—that is, a privatized—market is expected to extend individual liberties and to promote democratic forms of government.

However, the global dominance of this perspective was not achieved through democratic processes. How a singular viewpoint gains the status of "knowledge" is a result of conflicting social forces. That is, "knowledge is not gained prior to and independent of the use to which it will be put in order to achieve power (whether over nature or over people), but is already a function of human interests and power relations."[2] Consequently, neoliberal globalization policies are political, shaped by particular interests and their privileged location within shifting power relations. They support a particular economic form that represents the interests and perspectives of the privileged. They are not simply the natural extension of trade.

As an economic policy supported by the power of (north-) Western governments, neoliberal globalization provides an overarching pattern into which the internal policies, practices, and possibilities of differing nations and communities must somehow fit. Within any particular society, neoliberal policies will take specific shapes based on that culture's existing patterns of social relations. This interaction between neoliberal globalization policies and national or local social relations creates social and economic dislocation. As such it destabilizes the existing distribution of benefits and burdens within a society.

In this way neoliberal globalization, while seemingly quite distant from the daily lives of ordinary people, reaches into local neighborhoods and places new demands on people and their families in the privacy of their homes. Without going through democratic processes of debate and consensus, it becomes a "common sense," a taken-for-granted knowledge, in Antonio Gramsci's sense, and a discipline, as Michel Foucault used the term.[3] In Gramsci's view, hegemony is an ongoing process by which a ruling group comes to power and sustains its position by establishing what becomes "common sense." Foucault showed how the shared meanings and concepts that seem implicit to a society are in fact the experiences and views of a privileged social group that have become fixed and widely accepted even by those who may be disadvantaged by them. The more they become "self-evident," the more they and their origin in social conflict become transparent, invisible. They become a "common sense" that is exercised in small acts and socially approved ways of being.

Being a "common" sense, alternative social arrangements with which neoliberal globalization once competed become unthinkable. In the United States the norms of postindustrial, neoliberal capitalism have reconstituted our experiences of life, our daily practices, our sense of values, and our sense of self. This is illustrated by an increasing faith in the wisdom of economic rationality that places more and more social responsibilities—from public schools to prisons to welfare offices—in the hands of private, for-profit business. It is now common for business executives to become high-level government officials, and vice versa, as entrepreneurial virtues are assumed to be the only key to real progress.

At the same time, fewer decisions about what social goods are and how they should be produced and distributed are being made through a participatory, democratic process that is genuinely free to imagine and create an uncommon, common good. The common sense of neoliberal capitalism has virtually silenced, or co-opted, traditions that could articulate an alternative sense of social priorities, public goods, and of how to achieve them.[4] Moral reasons for placing limits on national economic growth, or on corporate practices, or on the individual pursuit of wealth seem quaint—somewhat out of touch with modern reality. The discussion of industrial democracy, the social wage, and living wages, prevalent in the 1930s and 1940s, has been silenced. In its place, the remark What's good for this country is good for General Motors, and vice versa, originally received as a horrendous gaffe, has become common sense.[5]

The New Economy

The "new economy" is the second contemporary economic context that changes the experience of the workplace and the family. That there is actually something new about the economy is contestable. Yet the term arises from a variety of locations. For example, *The Economic Report of the President, 2001*, states: "Over the last 8 years the American economy has transformed itself so radically that many believe we have witnessed the creation of a New Economy."[6] For Alan Greenspan, the chairman of the Federal Reserve, the term "new economy" refers to the expansion of information technology into every business sector so that decisions can be made more rapidly in response to the smallest market changes. It brings new speed to the old process of "creative destruction," in which new technologies replace old ones.[7]

As used here, "new economy" focuses on the transition in economic relationships that characterizes business practices in the era of neoliberal globalization. How the new economy will change the relation of employer to employee provides an example. In the United States, a nineteenth-century court decision declared, "All may dismiss their employee(s) at will, be they many or few, for good cause, for no cause, or even for a cause morally wrong."[8] This represented the "employment-at-will" doctrine and practice that interpreted employment as a contractual arrangement between two independent parties. Either party had the right to terminate the contract at its sole discretion. In the last hundred years, this absolute right of employers has been gradually restricted in response to the recognition that employees typically suffer more from loss of work than an employer suffers from loss of an employee. During and after World War II, unionized work and government employment usually protected workers' job security by requiring that firing be "for cause."

Where employees were not so protected, that is, in most private employment, the courts began to offer some protection. In 1980, two Michigan cases were tried in which the employees argued that they had been given assurances when they were hired that as long as they did a good job, they would have a job. In upholding the employees' claims, the court observed that while an employer need not make such promises, such promises are in fact beneficial to both parties. "The employer secures an orderly, cooperative and loyal work force, and the employee the peace of mind associated with job security and the conviction that he will be treated fairly."[9] In the field of business ethics, a consensus has also developed that fairness requires that employees not be fired arbitrarily. One text on business ethics concludes, "When employers can dismiss at will, legitimate property rights of employees and the right of employees to contract freely are severely eroded." The author concludes: "Employment at will is, fortunately, an idea whose time is past."[10]

However, this reasoning is based on the logic of the old economy. One presumption behind this evolving limitation on employers' rights to take away employees' jobs was an economic rationale: while employers need to be free to follow their productive interests, productive employees, by definition, are assets to the company. In normal circumstances, loyalty between worker and employer benefits each party. Unless the firm's profitability and competitiveness are at stake, the firm's right to dismiss employees without cause and due process should be limited by employees' right to a reasonable expectation of job security. Thus, over the course of the twentieth century, courts have developed the concept that a job represents a property interest of employees that cannot be taken without due process and due cause.

The new economy, however, is based on a different rationale: skilled, productive, loyal, and responsible employees may not be economic assets to the company *at this moment*. In the new economy, firms must be able to react immediately to shifts in market conditions. Efficiency is crucial to survival. No job can be protected that does not make an immediate economic contribution. According to Peter Capelli, "The new paradigm is a wide-spread recognition that there are big cost savings if you do not have to carry workers and can get rid of them quickly when there is not enough for them to do."[11] Barbara Andolsen describes this as a shift from the evolving promise of job security in exchange for good work to the open recognition that "the employee has a job only as long as the employee's work promotes the company's immediate goals and enhances the company's short-term profitability."[12] Today, fully 90 percent of all workers in the private sector are employed "at-will"; that is, they are employed solely at the will of their employers, as employee manuals now make clear.[13]

Contexts for Women

Conditions of Injustice
Clearly, my motivation for this study has not been enthusiasm for the new economy. It has been fear: fear for women, mothers, and their children. The economist Lourdes Benería writes,

It is, in fact, ironic that as the world's capacity to produce and meet the basic needs of its population has reached unprecedented heights with modern technologies and economic globalization, some of the most basic human problems remain unresolved or have even deteriorated.[14]

These most basic human problems, unresolved and worsening, directly impact the lives of women and result in three conditions of injustice based on gender.

First, it is women and their children who constitute a disproportionate share of the human population living in want of adequate levels of health, nutrition, education, and opportunity—whose basic human needs go unmet in both overdeveloped countries and the countries of the two-thirds world.[15] A U.N. report released in 1992 found that little had changed in women's lives during the previous twenty-year period: "women continue to be a global underclass, working longer hours than men for less money, without sufficient access to education or medical care and with virtually no voice in government or industry."[16]

In the United States, the poor are also disproportionately women, children, and people of color. Economist Nancy Folbre has noted that being female and having a child in the United States creates the greatest risk of poverty. She calls this the "pauperization of motherhood."[17] Women's greater deprivation is not simply an issue of distributive justice. It is the result of a tangle of gendered political economic practices and beliefs from which women's assessment of their own interests has been excluded. It is an issue, then, of domination and oppression. The deeper ethical issue is political as well as economic as the new economy redefines "social relationships of power that exist in the human attempt to gain livelihood for the community and its members."[18] The economy is political. Creating justice for women, then, is a question of creating the conditions in all social institutions by which women can develop and exercise their human capacities and participate collectively in shaping those social conditions.[19]

Second, between 1970 and 1990 the presence of women grew rapidly in the ever-expanding global market for low-wage workers. There are at least one hundred export processing zones in the countries of the two-thirds world. Among scholars using gender analysis there is general agreement that "the preferred labor force in these zones is female, very young, and with little or no previous work experience."[20] Some may argue that there are positive dimensions to this development. Economically, the expansion of employment for wages is typically seen as synonymous with economic development. Rising standards of living require the production of more products. Increasing production requires economies of scale beyond the capacities of individual home production. Employment for wages provides the income by which to purchase new products, creating more demand. Furthermore, women's employment has the potential to destabilize traditional gender arrangements by giving women access to their own income, the experience of greater independence, and, thus, a better bargaining position with men in their households.

However, whether women's employment for wages actually enhances the equality of most women or the well-being of their families requires a much closer look at the material realities of women's employment. The clustering of women into low-wage work, the gap in income between women and men, and women's unrelieved responsibility for unpaid family labor may disrupt traditional gender roles. But it may also be creating new unequal ones. Suspicion of the latter lies behind this book's close look at the impact of women's wage employment on the goal of social equality for women.

Third, there is a growing global trend for women to be the sole head of the household, responsible for the well-being of their family. This is occurring at the same time that the cost of caring for children and other dependent persons is increasing. The extent of this problem is difficult to assess because of the lack of attention given to the issue by economists and because of the use of gendered assumptions about male and female relations within the household. In most global data collection, the presence of an adult male qualifies the household as headed by a male. Without examining the actual flow of income into the household, it is difficult to calculate the percentage of households maintained by one or more women, regardless of the presence of an adult male. Divorce and abandonment, economic migration, and out-of-wedlock births all contribute to the more visible proportions of this phenomenon. Between 1970 and 1990, the unwed birth rate went from 13 percent to 25 percent in Austria; from 11 percent to 47 percent in Denmark; from 7 percent to 32 percent in France. Over 45 percent of all births in Latin America were to unmarried women in 1990.[21] In most regions, the percentage of households headed by females exceeds 20 percent.[22] Seeing this trend in its broader global context suggests that the explanation of neoclassical economics, an explanation that emphasizes individual preferences and choices, is deeply flawed. It also suggests that there is more to the story than the explanation promoted by popular discourse in the United States about family values, that is, the triumph of self-interested individualism over parents' responsibility for their families.

The combination of these three conditions—poverty and social dis-empowerment, increased economic responsibility for family maintenance, and employment in low-wage work—creates a context in which most women of the world struggle to make a life for themselves and their families. Although no woman fully escapes the consequences of her gender, the intensity and cost of that struggle differ widely among women based on the opportunities and constraints of their class, race and ethnicity, nationality, sexual orientation, and age. In fact, a close look at women's differences suggests that the successful strategies of some depend on the constraints to which others are subject. Consequently, the goal to achieve women's equality will ultimately necessitate a more egalitarian vision of society as a whole, and, yes, it will need to be more egalitarian than the Christian tradition has to this point anticipated.

Women's Participation in the Work Force
Women's revised patterns of employment are, of course, connected to the practices of neoliberal globalization. These practices, interacting with local patterns of social relations, have brought about a new normative gender behavior and a new legitimating gender ideology. In the United States, the rate of participation of women in the labor force rose from 21 percent in 1920 to just over 60 percent in 2002.[23] During this sharp increase the proportion of U.S. women working part-time remained fairly constant at 20 percent.[24] Thus, this dramatic movement of women into the U.S. labor force was primarily a movement into full-time employment. Furthermore, this increase was most widespread among married women, and especially white married women. Neoliberal globalization, then, is a *gendered* economic transition that is reshaping the lives and roles of women and men and intrafamily relations.

In the United States, these economic forces found cultural support. For over two hundred years, U.S. feminists struggled against restrictive gender roles. Theirs is a history punctuated by moments of progress and moments of regression. Certainly this long history provided fertile cultural ground into which the new requirements of an economy being restructured by neoliberal globalization could fall. Certainly the impact of the civil rights movements of the 1960s and 1970s in the United States was an important factor in changing the common sense of society with regard to "women's work."[25] However, the worldwide phenomenon of women's entry into wage labor cannot be explained by the strength of national feminist movements, not even in the United States. Such a singular explanation ignores the diversity in women's experiences of wage work and the diversity of women's needs and options. It ignores the connections between the rise in service and clerical work for women in the United States and the recruitment of women around the world onto production lines. To understand what drives diverse women in differing contexts to enter the formal economy through wage work requires understanding how particular institutional responses shape women's options and how different households choose different mechanisms for maintaining themselves under changing and insecure conditions.

For example, it should not be assumed that the desire to break out of a patriarchal division of labor that assigned some women to domesticity was the motivation for all women, although it was certainly a motivation for some. In the United States the expansion of women's wage work is related to the stagnation in wages that most male workers have experienced since the 1970s. Such an economic change initiates conflict and reform in gender identities and roles, in productive and reproductive work, and in the survival strategies of families. It also creates new family stress around managing the care of children and other dependent persons. The constant fear of economic loss, the stress of conflict and change in gender roles, and increased concerns about care of dependents give rise to a real "family crisis," a crisis produced by neoliberalism's mantra of "economic rationality."

Nor should it be assumed that all women benefit equally from the revision of women's gender roles to include employed work. Ethical analysis must pay attention to differences based on race and class and other forms of socially structured difference, as well as to the relationships that exist between women in differing social locations. Some women and families may be able to achieve the new two-earner family ideal by purchasing products and services provided by poorly paid women. A feminist ethical analysis must admit and respond to the fact that the lives of more successful women, most of whom are white, are not simply different from the lives of women of other classes and races. Rather, they are systemically connected to the lives of economically poor women, a disproportionate share of whom are women of color.

Contexts for Families

The impact of neoliberal globalization and the new economy on women is a global phenomenon placing new demands on families and intrafamilial relations. Martin Carnoy argues that the traditional nuclear family is in decline in all the countries of the Organisation for Economic Co-operation and Development. He cites two primary causes: (1) women's rising expectations of equality, and (2) changes in the workplace of the global economy. Since he neither expects nor desires that either of these causes will be reversed, Carnoy argues for the provision of social supports for the "flexible" families developing in this economy.[26] I do not share his enthusiasm for the new flexible economy nor his sanguineness about its impact on families. But I find this analysis revealing the connection between economic forces and family forms helpful, although limited by lack of sufficient attention to class and race or ethnic differences within nations.

When mindful of economic forces, as well as race and class differences, the term "family crisis" should function as a critique of social systems that provide unmerited benefits for some at the unmerited expense of others. Some families have always been in crisis. Race discrimination is a family crisis. It always has been. Legislation passed in northeastern states between 1780 and 1804 for the purpose of gradually freeing black slaves required that the children of slave mothers continue to work as servants indentured to the master (now employer) for between eighteen and twenty-eight years. Surely these were families in crisis.[27]

Poverty, the condition in which parents are unable to provide the material goods, services, and opportunities needed for the full development of their children's individual capacities and for their own meaningful participation in society, has always been a family crisis. In the beginning of the twentieth century, 20 percent of U.S. children lived in orphanages. Their parents were not dead; they were simply too poor to take care of their children.[28] Surely, these were families in crisis. Today, in Michigan, half of 1,700 low-income families surveyed had lost time from work because of childcare problems, and almost half of their teenaged children were at home alone during some of the hours each day that their parents work.[29] For these families, life is constantly lived on the edge of crisis.

Today, however, the term "family crisis" is used differently. In popular discussions of the decline in virtue, family crisis is understood as an issue of individual moral behavior. According to this "common sense," divorce rates, single female heads of households, teen pregnancy, poverty, crime, drug addiction, low SAT scores, and other expressions of social degradation are caused by the collapse of moral character. All these ills and the lack of moral character that creates them are laid at the door of "families." The failure of families to do the work of families has spurred a call for renewing communities by establishing, through persuasion or legislation, a stronger standard of social morality. In *Coming Together/Coming Apart*, Elizabeth Bounds argues that the concern for "community" among academics, social intellectuals, and politicians is actually a response to the struggles going on within the institutions of civil society owing to the destabilizing impact of "modern advanced capitalism."[30]

Similarly, I focus on its impact on gender and family. To follow Bounds's insight, the discourse about family crisis is a trope for the conflicts that arise when gender relations and family forms become sites of struggle in response to the corrosive influence of economic transitions. Unfortunately, much of the current literature of family decline lacks any sort of socioeconomic analysis. While rightly critical of the individualism of liberalism, much of the concern about family values assumes that individuals and their families can simply resist the economic forces that are relentlessly reshaping their lives. While rightly calling for individuals to take up their responsibility for the quality of familial and communal life, there is no parallel call to hold the political economy responsible for its destruction of community and family life. It is, in words Beverly Harrison used to critique much of feminist theology and ethics today, "remote from the actual dynamics of our historical situatedness in a political economy which, as never before, is restructuring the lives and life conditions of every man, woman, and child on little planet earth."[31] In the current rhetoric of family crisis, therefore, the economy serves primarily as a given: an unproblematic, even positive, backdrop against which civil and family life is lived.

However, looking at the role of women and the family based on an analysis of the political economy enables one to ask different questions about women's equality and family values. How do families adjust to economic change, crisis, and instability? How does a culture's gendered division of labor shape women's roles and strategies for survival and resistance in the context of economic change? How are new gendered identities and a new justifying common sense created? Finally, this is the most fundamental ethical question: Does the nature and logic of advanced corporate capitalism, enhanced by a neoliberal political economy, support the values and policies necessary to provide equality among all women and well-being for all families?

METHODOLOGY

I address these questions out of the discipline of social ethics as understood from a Christian liberative and materialist feminist perspective. Material feminism, with its attention to the differences among women, extends Susan Moller Okin's argument that women's social location is one of "asymmetric vulnerability." Race and class further shape a gender inequality that, as socially constructed, is morally unjustified.[32] Moreover, material feminism attempts to understand how the social construction of modern and postmodern identities is bound up with, although not rigidly determined by, shifting needs of production under the logic of neoliberal, postindustrial capitalism. It provides a method for understanding the organic relations between home and work, between the reproduction of society and the production of material goods.

Basic to a Christian liberative and material feminist perspective is an understanding that a just society requires a material basis: that is, basic conditions of material well-being achieved through a society's commitment to all of its people are the precondition for meaningful political democracy. A Christian liberative ethics identifies those basic conditions of material well-being and seeks to move toward realizing them, taking into account the concrete realities and events that shape women's daily lives. The Roman Catholic social justice tradition is helpful in identifying the basic conditions of material well-being. According to that tradition, human rights include a number of economic rights, which for my purposes I will call specifically *women's* economic rights:

> ... the rights to life, food, clothing, shelter, rest, medical care, and basic education. . . . In order to ensure these necessities, all [*women*] have a right to earn a living, . . . a right to security in the event of sickness, unemployment and old age. Participation in the life of the community calls for the protection of the rights [of *women*] to employment, to healthful working conditions, to wages and other benefits sufficient to provide [*women*] and their families with a standard of living in keeping with human dignity, and to the possibility of property ownership. These fundamental [*women's*] rights— civil, political as well as social and economic—state the minimum conditions for social institutions that respect [*women's*] dignity, social solidarity and justice.[33]

However, rather than extending these basic conditions of material well-being, there is a growing acceptance in the United States of material inequality.[34] Wage inequality in the United States is greater today than it has been since the Great Depression and greater than in any other industrialized country. The top 20 percent of U.S. families receive almost 50 percent of the after-federal-tax income for all families. The top 1 percent of U.S. households own almost 40 percent of the nation's household wealth; the top 20 percent own 84 percent.[35] Such inequality severely truncates the practice of democracy in this country even as we pride ourselves on being a democratic ideal for other nations to duplicate. Decisions that impact questions of use of resources, educational needs, use of time, character values, parenting practices, knowledge and news productions, and so forth, are increasingly made within business structures that are not democratic. What is possible as political questions in public discourse, that is, questions of what sort of society we should be, is limited by the growing acceptance of many issues as merely economic. When issues are perceived as economic they are placed in the realm of privately owned, profit-oriented, business decision-making that is not responsible for mediating the interests of other aspects and institutions of human life.

The spread of economic reasoning is the result of the constantly deepening ideology of capitalism. "Ideology," which means a worldview, a cultural paradigm, or, as Robert Heilbroner puts it, "deeply and unselfconsciously held views," and explanatory systems of thought and belief, functions as both evidential truth and moral truth. A dominant ideology, or hegemonic ideology, is one that represents those "deeply and unselfconsciously held views of the dominant class in any social order." These are the views "by which dominant classes explain *to themselves* how their social system operates and what principles it exemplifies." [36] I agree with Heilbroner that the purpose of dominant ideologies is to clarify and enlighten everyone by providing a way to see that is normal—that is, to gain general acceptance of the way the dominant group sees and understands its own activities.[37] This is not to deny the variety of views that exist within a dominant worldview; it is to argue that these differences do not ultimately challenge the sources of unequal power relations. They typically justify in various ways the existence of deprivation and serve to limit what can be seriously contemplated.

But the concept of ideology is not limited to beliefs or views, as though ideas can be abstracted from experience. Ideology is a material force. Daily activities, institutional practices, internalized race-, class-, and gender-identities, styles of clothing, forms of entertainment, family habits, and so forth, all participate in a discursive totality through which we are *given* ourselves. A dominant ideology reproduces itself through social action— what is heard, seen, built, printed, valued, made, spoken, practiced—that is privileged as reality. Political, cultural, and economic activities all participate in this social reproduction. The power of a dominant ideology lies exactly in its embodied expression of that to which a dominant group is actually committed based on its experience of social life. We learn that ideology simply by learning to live properly in our culture. Amata Miller's phrase "cruel innocence" captures the sense of moral self-assurance that characterizes a dominant ideology with its power to limit the view of good people.[38] Assured of their innocence, members of a dominant group never see, much less question, the harm they bring to others.

The problem for ethics, then, is that good intentions are not sufficient. Within our own horizons, what does not fit will remain unseen, be ignored, or be considered abnormal. One task of Christian social ethics is to find ways to identify dominant ideologies that are present in our cultures and to clarify the interests, values, and social origins of these ideologies in the pattern of social relations. The methodology I use to identify dominant ideologies is necessarily interdisciplinary and dependent on the social sciences. Such an approach carries with it extraordinary challenges and dangers. The various social science theories are themselves divided by inter- and intradisciplinary disagreements and differing ideological commitments. An ethicist has to make choices among and within disciplines possibly without being fully proficient in any of them.

Moreover, for feminists, the issue goes beyond determining competence in disciplinary methodologies. In every field, feminist scholarship raises serious questions about the role that presuppositions and group interests play in shaping methods and in assessing data. The work of feminist scholars restructures the conclusions of the sciences as well as the questions; it challenges theories and also basic paradigms. While research for this book draws from many sources, my commitments to women's equality and the well-being of families shape my judgment of what seems problematic or reasonable or possible. For example, I turn to feminist economists who have rejected a value-free notion of economics and "view economic discourse as a social practice with concrete historical origins."[39] They join those economists interested in addressing more broadly the relationships between social structures and individual agents, between the economy and the rest of society, and between researchers and the objects of their research. Feminist economic analysis not only adds new topics for research. It challenges the theoretical and methodological bases of neoclassical and neoliberal economics.

COMMITMENTS

My interest and ethical commitments arise out of personal experience and feminist liberatory readings of the Christian tradition. My affinity to material feminism probably lies in my long-standing naïve inability to make sense of women's lives, including my own, without probing most women's unstable and always conditional relationship to material well-being.

I watched my mother's efforts to fulfill all her human capacities—as wife, mother of four (sometimes single mother during my father's military absences), organist, choir director, music teacher, and, finally, ordained minister. Upon my father's forced retirement from the military, part of troop cutbacks after the Korean War, my mother returned to her first career as a public school music teacher while continuing her work as a church musician. In the 1950s, her income needed to be added to that of my father's teaching salary in order to sustain a middle-income lifestyle for a family of six—or seven during the six months of the year that my grandmother lived with us. Her balancing act of unpaid domestic work and work for wages required enormous energy and commitment far beyond the eight-hour day or the five-day workweek. It also involved a much longer work life. Her career in ministry could not start until her children were raised. It did not become her profession until after the death of my father. Nonetheless, her ministry spanned twenty-some years before ending in retirement at the age of eighty-seven.

I am part of the next generation of white, middle-income women who were expected to get a college education before marrying. College provided a place to find suitable husbands and an education appropriate to our class. It also would be useful in case some unexpected tragedy would cause us to have to earn a living. For my generation—as with my mother's—working for wages for a few years after college typically preceded a long stay-at-home period of domesticity, raising children, followed by retirement—all dependent on a husband's wages, health insurance, and pension. Accepting the asymmetrical vulnerability of economic dependency was part of being white, female, and middle-income. This pattern, however, if not broken by other unexpected tragedies, has been increasingly broken by divorce. In my case, six years of participation in the work force were followed by fifteen years of domesticity before divorce revealed to me the skewed social rules. Even for middle-income, educated white women, divorce requires a return to employment. It also means starting anew at the lower rungs of the economic ladder—beginning a pension plan and social security contributions in mid-life and at a low-income level. For both my mother's generation and mine, caring for families meant accepting economic loss, unequal economic vulnerability with men, and unequal time for professional development.

Today my daughter assumes that income-producing work is integral to her life. She postponed marriage to pursue a professional education in the law. She does not envision or desire an end to her career. Yet, she must wrestle with how motherhood will impact the type and trajectory of that career. Should she stop working for a few years at childbirth? With each child? Or, should she try to work at least part-time? What type of law practice best lends itself to mothering? These are all questions that husbands, even good husbands, typically do not acknowledge as equally applicable to themselves. Or, in facing them, a couple intent upon achieving domestic equality recognizes that they cannot afford to strike an egalitarian balance between productive and reproductive work.[40] The way work is organized requires that one of them be a serious, full-time worker. Consequently, women still take on the greater risk of economic dependency in order to do the work of caregiving. Wage work and family work are still not compatible even for middle- and upper-income, professionally educated women unless unequal economic vulnerability for women is accepted as normal and just.

Economically poor women face far fewer options with even fewer resources. As each group of women chooses from the limited options available to them, the lives of both groups of women become connected. Gender, race, and class injustices intertwine. As Audre Lorde pointedly said to white feminists, more affluent white women often break covenant with poor women, who are more likely to be black or Hispanic.[41] Our lives are eased and our careers advanced by the labor of domestics, Merry Maids, Wal-Mart associates, and nurses' aides; theirs are not. This is the paradox in which personal choices become political acts. It is a matter of moral seeing.

There is also a paradox at the center of Christian faith. The heart of the Christian tradition is a faith-initiated moral imperative to respond to concrete human suffering in a manner that contributes to the construction of community wholeness. Protestants tend to use the Hebrew symbol of the covenant community to signify this vision of an inclusive and egalitarian way of relating to others, not only personally but especially through just social systems.

Yet, the heart of the Christian tradition also includes recognition of the brokenness of community. Unjust social relations may cause suffering, extend it, deny it, or refuse to respond to it. This is not simply a matter of individual selfishness, hubris, or greed (although such vices exist). It is not simply a matter of confronting and changing individual hearts (although that, too, is necessary). The profound brokenness that characterizes (post)modern human community and threatens all life on earth is at its depth a matter of changing social systems, a matter of doing justice, a matter of creating communities of equal regard.

> ... it is not enough to simply go to the human heart and find it wanting, driven by greed toward privileges and unwilling to accept responsibility. In addition, the systems of thought we use to analyze life and nature shape the conditions under which the earth suffers.[42]

Within a system of democratic capitalism, then, the task of Christian economic ethics must go beyond issues of distributive justice and consumerism. It must go once again to the question of participatory meaning-making, to the question of who is included in the community of world-shaping agents. Whose common sense participates in the shaping of the common good? And what social patterns of relationship should be produced by the political economy to justify and support the practice of democratic decision-making within a political economy? The concern that many ethicists have had in the past for the dangers of a coercive government now need to be expanded to recognize the dangers of a more subtle regime produced by an economy on which all depend.

This is not a new task. (North-) Western Christianity has developed ways of thinking about economic activities. The Protestant emphasis on covenantal relations within every sphere of life and the Roman Catholic emphasis on the basic entitlements necessary to fulfill the human *telos* assume that economic activities will be subordinate to, or at least harmonious with, a common good that recognizes a Christian "table of values."[43] In the nineteenth century and into the twentieth, these values led Christian voices to challenge absolute claims to private property, chattel slavery, *wage* slavery, and the use of Social Darwinism to justify economic exploitation.[44] Christian voices called for the democratization of both social and economic power.

However, since the Second World War, and especially with the collapse of the Soviet Union, the mainline debate within Christian ethics has *assumed* a capitalist paradigm. Differences among mainstream North American Christian ethicists are primarily located in differing assessments of (1) how effective the capitalist free-market system is with regard to distributive justice, and (2) what amount of state intervention is needed to attend to the needs of those harmed by or unable to participate in this market system.

At the turn of twenty-first century, the ethical imperatives of women's equality and the well-being of families raise again the question of the basic compatibility of capitalism and Christianity. Christian faithfulness is still most threatened by the acquiescence of those Christians in overdeveloped social locations to the powers that sustain our privileges at the expense of most other humans and all of nature. The concentration of economic power in the hands of the few must be loudly challenged. The singularity of economic viewpoint that dominates the United States and the process of globalization must be challenged. In ways that provoke our own action, we need to lament the loss of so much of humanity to the deprivation of poverty and the despair of exploitive work. We need to interrogate the savagely innocent materialism of the affluent. And we need to ask why women, mothers, and children, especially families of color, bear such a disproportionate share of suffering.

It is difficult to challenge that which has become so embedded in every social structure that its effects are often invisible to us or misidentified. However, it is a task central to feminist liberation theologies that see God's power forming a renewed creation: a new earth that is a "qualitatively different earth freed from kyriarchal exploitation and dehumanization."[45]

NOTES

1. Elisabeth Schüssler Fiorenza, *Jesus: Miriam's Child Sophia's Prophet: Critical Issues in Feminist Christology* (New York: Continuum, 1995), 7.

2. D. C. Hoy, "Power, Repression, Progress: Foucault, Lukes, and the Frankfurt School," in *Foucault: A Critical Reader*, ed. D. C. Hoy (Oxford: Basil Blackwell, 1986), 129.

3. Antonio Gramsci, *Selections from the Prison Notebooks of Antonio Gramsci*, ed. and trans. Quinton Hoare and Geoffrey Nowell Smith (New York: International Publishers, 1972); Michel Foucault, *The History of Sexuality*, trans. R. Hurley (New York: Vintage, 1980), 85f.

4. This exclusion of alternatives also exists within the community of international economists and political scientists where those who argue for different routes to well-being for different nations are ignored. See Jeff Madrick, "Economic Scene: The mainstream can't or won't recognize some basic facts about world poverty," *New York Times*, 2 August 2001: C2. These "dissenters" include, for example, Harvard economist Dani Rodrik, *The New Global Economy and Developing Countries: Making Openness Work* (Washington, D.C.: Overseas Development Council, 1999), and law professor Roberto Unger, *Democracy Realized: The Progressive Alternative* (New York: Verso Books, 1998). Co-optation of alternative values is a primary vehicle of advertising: for example, world unity based on drinking Coca Cola, and love expressed by the purchase of diamonds.

5. Bruce J. Schulman, "Is the Business of America Business?" *New York Times,* 13 May 2001: WK4. Schulman recounts how this remark, made by Eisenhower's secretary of defense, a former General Motors executive, was used to embarrass Eisenhower by his opponents for many years. Seeing the remark as inappropriate depends upon understanding the role of a democratic government to be the protection of social values that may be different from and in contention with the interests of private business.

6. *The Economic Report of the President, 2001,* 19; available at www.acess.gpo.gov/usbudget/fy2002/pdf/2001_erp.pdf.

7. Alan Greenspan, "Structural Changes in the New Economy," 7/11/2000: www.federalreserve.gov.

8. Quoted in Lawrence E. Blades, "Employment at Will versus Individual Freedom: On Limiting the Abusive Exercise of Employer Power," *Columbia Law Review* 67 (1967): 1405. Blades is citing *Paine v. Western & A.R.R.,* 81 Tenn. 507, 519–20 (1884).

9. *Toussaint* v. *Blue Cross and Blue Shield of Michigan* and *Ebling* v. *Masco Corporation,* 408 Mich. 579, 272 N.W. 2d 880 (1980), quoted in John R. Boatright, *Ethics and the Conduct of Business* (Englewood Cliffs, N.J.: Prentice Hall, 1993), 281.

10. Boatright, *Ethics and the Conduct of Business,* 282–83. Most texts on business ethics continue to discuss the give and take between the right of employers to conduct business rationally and the right of employees to a reasonable expectation of job security as long as they are performing adequately. The texts have not yet caught up with the ethical challenges of the new economy.

11. Quoted in Louis Uchitelle, "Pink Slip? Now, It's All in a Day's Work," *New York Times,* 5 August 2001: BU 1, BU 11. Capelli is professor of management and co-director of the Center for Human Resources at the Wharton School of the University of Pennsylvania.

12. Barbara Andolsen, *The New Job Contract: Economic Justice in an Age of Insecurity* (Cleveland: Pilgrim Press, 1998), 2

13. Nelson Lichtenstein, *State of the Union: A Century of American Labor* (Princeton, N.J.: Princeton University Press, 2002), 3.

14. Lourdes Benería, "Preface," in *Unequal Burden: Economic Crises, Persistent Poverty, and Women's Work,* ed. Lourdes Benería and Shelley Feldman (Boulder, Colo.: Westview Press, 1992), viii.

15. Terms such as "first-world," "third-world," "developed nations," and "undeveloped" or "underdeveloped nations" all participate in the common sense of neoliberal capitalism. They promote the assumption of universal national progress led by the Western colonial nations with all other nations making progress to the extent that they adopt neoliberal capitalism. The phrase "two-thirds world" describes a different relationship—one between overdeveloped sectors and peripheral sectors. The overdevelopment of some comes at the expense of the periphery whose human and natural resources serve the interests of over-

development. The periphery, the two-thirds world, is not defined by national boundaries but by people's relationship to material resources.

16. "The World's Women: Trends and Statistics 1970–1990," cited in Claire Badaracco, "Can the Church Save Women? Public Opinion, the U.N. and the Policy Gap," *America*, 14 March 1992: 215.

17. Quoted in Randy Albelda and Chris Tilly, *Glass Ceilings and Bottomless Pits: Women's Work, Women's Poverty* (Boston: South End Press, 1997), 24.

18. M. Douglas Meeks, *God the Economist: The Doctrine of God and Political Economy* (Minneapolis: Fortress Press, 1989), xi.

19. Iris Marion Young, *Justice and the Politics of Difference* (Princeton, N.J.: Princeton University Press, 1990), 37. That social justice requires effective participation within one's community is also part of the Roman Catholic tradition. See David Hollenbach, "The Bishops and the US Economy," *Theological Studies* 46 (1985): 109.

20. Altha J. Cravey, *Women and Work in Mexico's Maquiladoras* (New York: Rowman & Littlefield, 1998), 6.

21. Sharlene Hesse-Biber and Gregg Lee Carter, *Working Women in America: Split Dreams* (New York: Oxford University Press, 2000), 62.

22. Susan Bullock, *Women and Work* (London: Zed Books, 1994), 17. O'Connell reports that "at least 30 percent of all households globally" are "women-maintained," that is, "either no adult male is present or if one is he contributes little or nothing to the household income" (*Women and the Family* [London: Zed Books, 1994], 67).

23. Teresa Amott and Julie Matthaei, *Race, Gender, and Work: A Multi-Cultural Economic History of Women in the United States*, rev. ed. (Boston: South End Press, 1996), 307; U.S. Bureau of Labor Statistics Data, "Labor Force Participation Rate—Civilian Population Female," 22 April 2002: www.bls.gov.

24. Martin Carnoy, *Sustaining the New Economy: Work, Family, and Community in the Information Age* (New York: Russell Sage Foundation, 2000), 31–32.

25. Terms such as wage work, productive work, the work of social re-production, unpaid labor, family work, and so forth, are attempts to carry out an analysis that contradicts the commonsense definition of "work," which is limited to those activities producing something to sell.

26. Carnoy, *Sustaining the New Economy*, 108–9. In 2000, the countries in OECD were Australia, Austria, Belgium, Canada, Czech Republic, Denmark, Finland, France, Germany, Greece, Hungary, Iceland, Ireland, Italy, Japan, Luxembourg, Mexico, Netherlands, New Zealand, Norway, Poland, Portugal, South Korea, Spain, Sweden, Switzerland, Turkey, United Kingdom, and the United States.

27. Jacqueline Jones, *American Work: Four Centuries of Black and White Labor* (New York: W. W. Norton, 1998), 163–64.

28. Stephanie Coontz, *The Way We Never Were: American Families and the Nostalgia Trap* (New York: Basic Books, 1992), 4.

29. Michigan Assemblies Project, *Welfare Reform: How Families Are Faring in*

Michigan's Local Communities (Detroit: Groundwork for a Just World, 1998), 21–27.

30. Elizabeth M. Bounds, *Coming Together/Coming Apart: Religion, Community, and Modernity* (New York: Routledge, 1997), 3.

31. Beverly Harrison, "Foreword," in Elizabeth Bounds, Pamela Brubaker, and Mary Hobgood, eds. *Welfare Policy: Feminist Critiques* (Cleveland: Pilgrim Press, 1999), vii.

32. Rosemary Hennessy and Chrys Ingraham, eds. *Material Feminism: A Reader in Class, Difference, and Women's Lives* (New York: Routledge, 1997); Susan Moller Okin, *Justice, Gender, and the Family* (New York: Basic Books, 1989), chap. 7. Although Okin is focused most explicitly on the asymmetrical vulnerabilities created by heterosexual marriage, her appropriation and extension of Robert Goodin's moral argument that socially constructed burdens of unequal vulnerability are unjust can itself be appropriated and extended to cast light on other forms of socially created unequal vulnerabilities such as class and race differences among women.

33. National Conference of Catholic Bishops, *Economic Justice for All: Pastoral Letter on Catholic Social Teaching and the U.S. Economy* (Washington, D.C.: U.S. Catholic Conference, 1986), para. 80. I recognize that by testing the bishops' use of gender-neutral language in this way consequences are suggested with which the bishops themselves may not fully agree. The specific insertion of women into what claims to be gender-neutral language often reveals gender-specific limits. For a careful justification of the argument for economic rights, see Darryl M. Trimiew, *God Bless the Child That's Got Its Own: The Economic Rights Debate* (Atlanta: Scholars Press, 1997).

34. Chuck Collins, Betsy Leondar-Wright, and Holly Sklar, *Shifting Fortunes: The Perils of the Growing American Wealth Gap* (Boston: United for a Fair Economy, 1999), 5; Edward N. Wolff, *Top Heavy: The Increasing Inequality of Wealth in America and What Can Be Done About It* (New York: New Press, 1996).

35. Lawrence Mishel, Jared Bernstein, John Schmitt, *The State of Working America 2000–2001* (Ithaca, N.Y.: Cornell University Press, 2001), 61, 260.

36. Robert Heilbroner, *The Nature and Logic of Capitalism* (New York: W. W. Norton, 1985), 107 (emphasis in the original).

37. Gloria Albrecht, *The Character of Our Communities: Toward an Ethic of Liberation for the Church* (Nashville: Abingdon Press, 1995).

38. Amata Miller, "Global Economic Structures: Their Human Implications," in *Religion and Economic Justice*, ed. Michael Zweig (Philadelphia: Temple University Press, 1991), 164. Miller is borrowing the phrase from Michael Harrington, who identified the suffering of the world's poor as conditional on good people's unawareness of their role within an economic system that ties us all together.

39. Ellen Mutari and Heather Boushey, "Introduction: The Development of Feminist Political Economy," in *Gender and Political Economy: Incorporating Diversity into Theory and Practice* (Armonk, N.Y.: Sharpe, 1997), 3.

40. See Pepper Schwartz, *Love Between Equals: How Peer Marriage Really Works* (New York: Free Press, 1995).

41. Audre Lorde, *Sister Outsider: Essays and Speeches by Audre Lorde* (Freedom, Calif.: Crossing Press, 1984), 112.

42. Paul G. King and David O. Woodyard, *Liberating Nature: Theology and Economics in a New Order* (Cleveland: Pilgrim Press, 1999), 16.

43. William Schweiker, "Responsibility in the World of Mammon," in *Religion and the Powers of the Common Life,* ed. Max L. Stackhouse and Peter J. Paris (Harrisburg, Penn.: Trinity Press International, 2000), 115.

44. See Max L. Stackhouse, *Public Theology and Political Economy: Christian Stewardship in Modern Society* (Grand Rapids, Mich.: Eerdmans, 1987), 36–51.

45. Elisabeth Schüssler Fiorenza, *Jesus,* 27.

2

Now that Women Work . . .

But today I see more clearly than yesterday that back of the problem of race and color, lies a greater problem which both obscures and implements it: and that is the fact that so many civilized persons are willing to live in comfort even if the price of this is poverty, ignorance and disease of the majority of their fellowmen.[1]

*T*HIS CHAPTER PRESENTS a brief history of the relationships that have existed in the United States between women and work. As with all histories, this account is selective. My interest is to illustrate how women's relationships with work have impacted and been impacted by gender identities, gender roles, and family formations as these are further shaped by race and economic location. In order to understand women's relationships to work, the meaning of terms that may seem quite simple and straightforward, such as "work," must be questioned.

"Do you work?" Fifty years ago this question put to a white woman was considered impolite. Wives working in the labor force implied a failed husband. It implied children running wild and unsupervised. It implied family dysfunction. Married women in good families did not work.[2] The question was simply inane, at least among middle- and upper-income married, white women. No one "like us" worked. What would cause anyone to ask such a question? Today Betty Friedan's 1963 book *The Feminine Mystique* is considered a feminist classic for highlighting the hidden discontent of this privileged group of women. *The Feminine Mystique* articulated in popular form the problem that lay beneath the placid surface of so many domestic, suburban, educated, white housewives in the '50s: what Friedan called, "the problem that has no name."

If I am right, the problem that has no name stirring in the minds of so many American women today is not a matter of loss of femininity or too much education, or the demands of domesticity. It is far more important than anyone recognizes. It is the key to these other new and old problems which have been torturing women and their husbands and children, and puzzling their doctors and educators for years. It may well be the key to our future as a nation and a culture. We can no longer ignore that voice within women that says: "I want something more than my husband and my children and my home."[3]

Twenty years later, in 1983, Friedan described the strong reaction she continued to receive from those who had read her book. Women and men still approached her to say exactly where they were when they first read the book, and how it changed their lives.[4]

Today, with the influx of white married women into the wage labor force, the question "Do you work?" is generally considered more reasonable and less pejorative. However, it continues to be a gendered one with no good answer for women who are mothers. Any mother's answer is often interpreted as revealing her position in a still contentious cultural debate over staying-at-home and going-to-work mothers. Mothers, but not fathers, feel the need to explain their work choices, often arguing that personal realities shape their decisions regardless of ideological commitments. The ideology of gendered roles and spaces persists within personal identities, social expectations, and institutional structures despite the material reality of women's lives.

Today, the questioner also runs a new risk of appearing insensitive to women's political struggles. Women have declared that the work they do, whether or not they are paid for it directly, is work.[5] Almost two decades ago, the United Nations reported that women perform nearly two-thirds of the work done in the world. While women are only one-third of the world's official labor force, they do virtually all of the domestic work, grow half the world's food, and provide more health care than all the health services.[6] Women work. Women have always worked. Yet, in the United States, the question "Do you work?" asked of women continues to display the common sense of a culture strongly shaped by an ideology that defines activities done at home to maintain the household as "not-work" and women as sometimes-workers. How "work" became defined (and is defined) was not a natural process. It was a process of social struggle with unjust consequences for all women.

Consequently, an adequate ethical concern for family well-being and gender equality must recognize that gender, family, and work are socially

constructed sites of relationships. Here the values of a capitalist logic inter-
act with, and often conflict with, other social values. These processes and
conflicts need to be exposed in order to subject them to ethical analysis.
Therefore, the following selective history of women's relationships to work
in the United States serves several purposes: (1) to examine the social construction of the current common sense that interprets work, family, and
gender; (2) to identify the interplay of racial, gendered, and economic
interests that participated in this construction and its re-construction;
(3) to display the organic and interlocking nature of the economic, cultural, and political arenas of society as they have constructed women's differing lives; and (4) to expose the material relationship that exists between
those who benefit from this social formation and those who do not.

A BRIEF HISTORY

The Disappearance of White Women's Work

Seventeenth and Eighteenth Centuries
In her book *Home and Work*, historian Jeanne Boydston addresses a paradox that has characterized women and work for most of U.S. history.[7] On
the one hand, women's very hard work has been essential to the survival
and prosperity of households; and, on the other, society's prevailing ideology, internalized by many women, denied that women's labors had any
economic value. Boydston provides an account of the origin and evolution
of this paradox in the Northeast, from colonial days to the Civil War. Her
aim is to explain the relationship between the actual material value of
women's work and the status it was given in society. Does the economic
importance of work determine its political and social status? Or, does
existing political and social status define what is considered economically
important? How does economic change impact gender relations and family forms? How do gender relations and family forms impact the organization of work?

In the early seventeenth century, the agrarian work of these women and
men of British and Dutch heritage roughly followed a spatial division of
labor. Men worked the outlying fields; women worked in the more immediate vicinity of the house. The production of each was essential to the
well-being of the family. Women provided fruits, vegetables, dairy products, and fowl. They manufactured goods for the family and sold or
bartered the surplus in local markets in exchange for other family needs.

They sewed, knitted, quilted, and spun; they prepared, cooked, and preserved foods. They also took in boarders and participated in their husbands' trades, often managing them after his death.

The households of property owners included many persons who were not relatives, such as servants and apprentices, as well as many children and step-children. All were part of what Stephanie Coontz calls "the corporate nature of family life."[8] Households were the basis of the production of products, of education and training for biological children and apprenticed children, for religious education, and for neighborly support of other families. Class divisions were experienced within households because most "propertyless people were dependents in a propertied household—wives, children, slaves, servants, apprentices, journeymen, hired laborers."[9]

Quoting a 1631 sermon titled "Economie" and subtitled "Or, Household-Government: A Short Survey of the Right Manner of Erecting and Ordering a Family, according to the Scriptures," by William Perkins, a Puritan minister, Boydston concludes, "All labor that contributed to the material viability of family life—whether it was growing food or cooking it, tending livestock or tending children—was 'economic.'"[10] Thus, for these colonists in the seventeenth century, work activities were delegated by gender; but "labor" was a gender-neutral term. Women and men labored. Both labored in the "economy."

However, ownership of property was a masculine prerogative. Women were valued as workers. The "good wife" of a property-owning husband exercised authority over servants, apprentices, and children, even though she was dependent on and subordinate to husbands, fathers, ministers, and magistrates in a society where the tools of social power were held by men. Women's subordination, as well as other unequal relationships, was explained as necessary to a social order divinely established. It was not attributed to women's biological and emotional attributes.[11]

White women's experience of work and its continued importance to household survival in that region did not change in the following century. The eighteenth-century household remained the center of economic production in the Northeast colonies. But other events were changing the experience of work for growing numbers of white men. As the availability of inheritable farmlands declined, younger sons began to swell the numbers of men who did not own property in a culture that identified property ownership with manhood. Population growth, coupled with wars that slowed the movement west, increased the size of towns and heightened competition among landless men for economic opportunities.

While barter remained the main form of exchange, money, traditionally controlled by male heads of households, began to be used more frequently for the payment of labor and goods. The need for cash income caused many households to participate in the "putting-out" system of production that included all household members as economic producers.[12] These changes gradually increased the visibility of money and initiated families' growing dependence on making money. Boydston notes that the impact of this economic evolution was also ideological. The emerging symbols of economic power were rooted in traditional masculine prerogatives separated from women's work: legal ownership of property, control of the family's cash income (regardless of who earned it), and the new self-interested, profit-oriented, market activity (now differentiated from activities that directly provisioned the family).

A new meaning of economy (once the "household") was emerging from real socioeconomic transformations, a meaning that focused narrowly on profit-motivated work outside the household. In the mid-eighteenth century Jared Eliot concluded that the profit incentive was what separated activity that was "work" from indolence.[13] Thus, despite women's ongoing, essential, provisioning activities, women no longer "worked," economically speaking. One minister found the value of (white) wives in their "wise Advices, their faithful Admonitions, their holy Examples, their devout Prayers, and *Labours of Love*."[14] It is important to keep in mind that this ideological transition was not necessitated by these actual economic changes. It was necessitated by patriarchal assumptions that named new forms of social authority masculine.

Boydston has shown that in the seventeenth century, white women's valued economic work did not result in greater social or political status for them. In the eighteenth century, as economic conditions changed for white men, what was economically valued also changed to reflect masculine prerogatives rather than the actual material contributions that women and men made to the family. The meaning, value, and status of work, family, men, and women were being redefined by a patriarchal society undergoing economic transformation.

Similarly, economist Julie Matthaei concludes from her study of women and work in the United States that the social status of the worker is not determined by the material importance of the work to the economy. Rather, work activities are given a social meaning within a set of social relationships (including race, gender, and class relationships) particular to a place and time. The social relationships that constitute economic processes produce a product. But they also produce a meaning of "work" and "worker" that justifies those social relationships. Thus, it was not the actual nature of women's activities that made white women nonworkers and their activities not-work. In the intersection of an expanding capitalism with a preexisting gendered system, masculinity was reprivileged as it assumed identity with these new, socially more powerful, economic activities. This, in turn, feminized the provisioning activities in the household.[15] A changing economy, being regendered, sired an ideology that denied economic value to white women's roles. This happened well before industrialization created for some white families, in the first half of the nineteenth century, an actual spatial separation between the masculinized location of market-product production and the feminized location of home production.

Nineteenth Century

The work of Boydston, Matthaei, Coontz, and others is part of a growing reconsideration of the history of gendered space: private (home, leisured, and feminine) and public (workplace, labored, and masculine). While this concept of separate gendered spaces has been useful to feminists characterizing the social and political limitations of white women in the nineteenth century, it is not adequate for describing what were more complicated gender, racial, and class relations. In its typical form, the theory of separate gendered spheres identified industrialization in the first half of the 1800s as the event that took activities of economic production out of the home (making them "public") while leaving only "private" activities related to reproduction and personal relationships in the feminine sphere of home. The theory often implies that the new availability of store-bought goods greatly reduced household activities and the necessity for skilled domestic labor.

This popular account is inaccurate in several ways. As we have seen, a change in economic ideology predates industrialization. Pre-existing masculine prerogatives supported the masculinizing of new profit-focused, cash-earning, economic activities. Production activities in the eighteenth-century household became labeled noneconomic because, as Boydston summarizes, concepts of gender "shape our perceptions of what constitutes work, who is working, and of the value of that labor."[16]

Further, industrialization did not end productive labor even in the white, middle-income homes of the nineteenth century. It transformed home work as it transformed the family. New tasks were added to old ones while the number of related people at home to participate in household work decreased. For example, in the seventeenth and eighteenth centuries, husbands did a good deal of the marketing. With industrialization, marketing in urban, middle-income homes became more complicated and more essential to the family. But, at the same time, middle-income husbands, developing a new identity as breadwinners, found shopping incompatible with their schedule of work hours. Consequently, middle-income wives took responsibility for daily shopping trips that involved dealing with people they were less likely to know, for goods whose quality was more difficult to assess.

Similarly, childrearing, a shared task in previous centuries for which fathers were ultimately responsible as the moral leaders of the family, became the responsibility of mothers. This happened at a time when the educational needs of middle-income children created a new, lengthy period of "childhood." Mothers, into whose hands the formation of moral and intellectual character was placed, were said to control "the destinies of a nation."[17]

The new technologies available to some middle-income families also changed the activities of the household but did not reduce them. Industrialization made manufactured cloth more accessible and, with the sewing machine, raised expectations about the amount of clothes that a good family should have. An increase in cooking tools and utensils made multiple-dish meals possible and also, by the end of the nineteenth century, created a new middle-class standard for meals.[18] As standards of class became more important for a newly emerging class of middle-income families, so activities that produced the symbols of middle-class status expanded.

Yet the paradox remained. Married white women did not and should not "work" and good wives were not "workers." Boydston illustrates the paradox for middle-income families with a letter that Harriet Beecher Stowe wrote to her sister-in-law, Sarah Beecher:

> Since her arrival with the children, she explained, she had "made two sofas—or lounges—a barrel chair—divers bedspreads—pillowcases—pillows—bolsters—mattresses . . . painted rooms . . . revarnished furniture." She had also laid a month-long siege at the landlord's door, lobbying him to install a new sink. Meanwhile, she had given birth to her eighth child, made her way through the novels of Sir Walter Scott, and tried to meet the obligations of her increasingly active career as an author—all of this while also attending to the more mundane work of running a household: dealing with tradespeople, cooking, and taking care of the children. . . . "And yet," she confided to her sister-in-law, "I am constantly pursued and haunted by the idea that I don't do anything."[19]

Nineteenth-century white, middle-income wives worked. Yet, by defining work as paid labor, their unpaid provisioning activities were redefined and rendered invisible as work.

In the literature of the day, home became "one place of sweet repose . . . of calm and sunshine amid the lowering storm. . . ." Food, clothing, furniture, cleanliness, medications, and healthy children appear without effort while woman keep

> that bright paradise, his home, . . . whose genial light kindles with soft and heavenly radiance upon the scene of loveliness which invites him to rest. With what refreshing gladness does he retire from the noise, and strife, and selfishness of the gentile court, into this *sanctum sanctorum* of the world's vast temple.[20]

Noise, strife, selfishness, and a lowering storm—all these describe the godless world of wage work.[21] The harms and threats deemed natural in the business world, the dehumanization of godless relationships, were to be healed in, and kept at bay from, the haven of home.

The creation of this refuge from masculine work thus necessitated the creation of a new gender. It was to be one marked by selected traits: nurturing, modesty of needs, fragility, spiritual focus, and moral purity. Yet, the ideology of gendered difference had little to do with the material existence of most women. According to historian Carroll Smith-Rosenberg, the discontinuity between the ideology of the "true woman," one who is gentle, dependent, fragile, spiritual, and so forth, and the realities of her adult responsibilities produced a number of women who reacted with the symptoms that were labeled "hysteria," one of the classic diseases of the nineteenth century that was peculiarly female.[22]

A feminist analysis does not assume that these gender arrangements were inevitable or uncontested. Instead, it asks what purpose this gender ideology, produced by middle- and upper-income white families, served at those sites of intersection between the logic of capitalism, racism, male dominance, and other social values. The answer requires recognition of the interrelationship between these lives and the lives of others.

As white women's identity was remade, so also white masculine identity was being re-formed. For skilled and unskilled white male workers, industrialization, new technologies, and the expansion of the wage system disrupted traditional relationships of production. Economic power was relocated and the rewards of labor redistributed. Industrialization eroded those roles and capacities that had been a source of masculine identity: pride in and control over one's product, ownership of property, and the provisioning of sons with the tools and skills by which they would also become men. This did not mean a change in work ethic. It meant conflict over "whom they were working for, at what pace, and by whose standards."[23]

As the artisan system declined, skilled work was divided into smaller pieces. Less-skilled workers could be quickly trained and as quickly replaced. By 1850, 50 percent of the craftsmen and women in New York City were employed as outworkers doing piecework in their own homes or in the small shops of subcontractors. The older hierarchical relationships between master craftsman and slave, indentured servant, apprentice, or journeyman were transformed into the new discipline of employer and employee, each "free." One was free to accept and leave employment, and one was free to hire and fire at will.

Almost totally dependent on wages, urban outworkers were buffeted by business cycles and the whims of supervisors who could reduce or withhold wages at will. Machinery increased the pace of work, and so did declining piece-rates. In 1850 the *New York Times* estimated that a subsistence income for a family of four in New York was $600 a year. Yet, the average annual income of white male tradesmen was only $300.[24] Class divisions once experienced within the household, divisions often related to age, skill, and experience, were now experienced between households. White male workers who once may have anticipated becoming peers with skilled craftsmen now were permanent wage earners subject to the flux of business cycles.[25]

Despite the rhetoric of a free labor market, historical studies of occupational mobility in the nineteenth century show that very few laborers, or their children, experienced the promised upward mobility.[26] Very detailed personnel records at the Amoskeag Textile Mills in Manchester, New Hampshire, reveal that 73 percent of the skilled workers experienced no change in the course of their careers. Of unskilled workers, 59 percent experienced no change. The records document laborers leaving the mills for what they hoped would be a way out of mill life with its limited opportunities for advancement, only to return. The mill provided more job stability than other working-class options throughout the nineteenth century and even better pay—though never enough to support a family on one wage.

The new wage system was not accomplished without resistance. When a judge in New York outlawed unions, calling them a restraint to trade, twenty-seven thousand people gathered at City Hall Park to denounce the decision.[27] Throughout the nineteenth century "mill girls" were active in labor organizing, calling for work stoppage and fighting for legislative relief from horrendous working conditions.[28] In less than fifty years from the signing of the Declaration of Independence, an urban, working-class consciousness had emerged in the Northeast, fragmented as it was by race/ethnicity and gender. Zinn summarizes:

> The new industrialism, the crowded cities, the long hours in the factories, the sudden economic crises leading to high prices and lost jobs, the lack of food and water, the freezing winters, the hot tenements in the summer, the epidemics of disease, the deaths of children—these led to sporadic reactions from the poor. Sometimes there were spontaneous, unorganized uprisings against the rich. Sometimes the anger was deflected into racial hatred for blacks, religious warfare against Catholics, nativist fury against immigrants. Sometimes it was organized into demonstrations and strikes.[29]

Under these harsh conditions, earning cash was an essential responsibility for poor and working-class northern women. They sold their domestic skills doing outwork as needle women and urban pieceworkers. They took boarders and laundry into already cramped tenements. Some left home to work as cooks and laundresses for crews digging canals and roads. Responsible for childcare, poor women and their children went into the street economy, where they were actors in the art of street commerce: rag pickers, street vendors, and hucksters. As scavengers they might blur the line between finding and stealing. Boydston reports that women regularly appeared in crime reports accused of stealing the necessities of family life—washtubs, clothing, pans, kettles. Displaced by industrialization from older means of support, such as spinning, and loath to enter the low-paid and extremely vulnerable work of domestic service, poor women also became more visible on urban streets as prostitutes.[30]

In the Northeast, as in the South, white women and children "manned" the textile mills. Jones describes the organization of poor women and children into work houses for the manufacturing of textiles as early as the mid-1700s. These work houses, such as the Philadelphia Bettering House, were justified by the affluent as charitable enterprises intended to uplift the idle poor while earning a return to the investors.[31] Goldin reports that the "the proportion of all young women in the northeastern states employed in the industrial sector was considerable as early as 1832 and rose rapidly wherever significant industrial development spread" until they comprised "about 40% of the entire industrial labor force around 1840."[32] Hareven describes how these northern mill girls were ultimately replaced by an even cheaper source of labor—entire immigrant families: French Canadian, Irish, and Italian.[33]

In the nineteenth century, the new ideal image of an insular, nuclear family that focused all its energy on preparing its children to succeed—with success defined as rising in social and economic status—was an image achieved only by urban, white, middle- and upper-income families. Poor, white, laboring people survived urban poverty in the Northeast as they survived rural poverty—extended families functioned as economic units.

Hareven's research of the Amoskeag Mills provides several insights into the experiences of working-class family life as a site of economic survival, contradicting and resisting middle- and upper-income gender and family norms. Wives and children as young as twelve (despite the law setting fourteen as the age of employment) went to work in the mills. For poor and working-class families, children's domestic work and wage work were essential to family survival, often at the cost of education. Out of economic need, children dropped out of school, or were sent to live for a length of time with relatives elsewhere. Marriages were delayed to keep older children's income supporting the family's younger children. Married children took up separate residences but remained close by. An informal family patronage system found mill jobs for relatives. Production skills were taught to kin. Men, women, and children all worked for wages, often with the same employer. In fact, because of the instability of manufacturing work, wives often became the major supporters of their families by taking the lowest status jobs or crossing picket lines.[34]

When contemporary discourse about family values makes the small nuclear family appear universal—or the universal goal of modern development—it ignores the differences in family arrangements that have always resulted from different access to economic resources. As we have seen, a pre-industrial, collective kinship system was pervasive among poor nineteenth-century urban families. Indeed, this made them the target of social reform movements late in that century. These family alternatives continue to persist into the twentieth and twenty-first centuries for poor and working-class people. Even today kin assistance might hamper the "success" of individual family members who are expected to place family needs above the pursuit of individualistic goals in life. But this kinship system enables families to survive inadequate wages, business cycles and job insecurity, accidents, ill health, and childbirth when neither government nor business accepts responsibility for the impact of poverty-wage labor on families.[35]

In contrast to the individualized family of the more affluent, then, the working-class families of the nineteenth century did not separate the family (that specialized feminine location of consumption, procreation, and childrearing for middle-income families) from work (that masculine site of production). Consequently, features of some families' lives became associated with lack of economic success: having nonrelatives living in the household such as boarders, having other relatives living in the household, being headed by a female, and having mothers leave home to do work for wages.

However, working white mothers, whether married or widowed or deserted or single, typically were not valued for their efforts to insure family survival. As early as the antebellum period, married white women in paid work began to be described as unnatural and were accused of taking away men's opportunities to provide for their families. By the end of the nineteenth century, even working-class men accepted the prevailing ideology of separate and gendered spheres. Their masculine identity had been redefined to focus almost exclusively on their ability to earn a wage, to be a breadwinner, in the public and masculine sphere of paid work.[36] By the beginning of the twentieth century, in the eyes of the dominant gender ideology, working mothers, sometimes even working wives, were signs of shameful indigence that often confirmed ethnic prejudices. According to the white feminist reformers of the time, working mothers were responsible for child abuse, child neglect, delinquency, truancy, and even the desertion of husbands.[37]

In the first half of the twentieth century, the ideology that defined white women as domestic and that identified families of wage-earning mothers as dysfunctional permeated personal identities and institutional structures. A 1923 study of poverty-level families found a labor participation rate of 96.3 percent for fathers, 96.6 percent for sons, 95 percent for unmarried daughters, and 25.9 percent for wives.[38] Employment opportunities for married white women, severely proscribed by both customs and traditions embodied in the preferences of employers, employees, and customers, were further limited by laws and company policies referred to as marriage bars.[39] Good married women did not "work" outside the home or within it. White women's work had disappeared.

The issue is definitional and political. In 1900, the U.S. Census did not count work done at home as work unless it provided most of the family's support. Caring for boarders, selling eggs, sewing and laundering for pay, and working in her husband's business were not work. All the unpaid but essential activities that enabled families to survive despite inadequate wages were invisible to economics. Sociologist Christine Bose calculates that if married women's income-producing household work, their employment in family-owned businesses and farms, and their wage work were counted, women's labor participation rate in 1900 would be between

48.5 percent and 56.7 percent (comparable to the rate of 54.5 percent in 1985).[40] But when work performed by women in the home to sustain family well-being is seen by men as an extension of women's gendered nature to provide domestic care, "good" women can be defined as nonworkers.

It is in this context that the labor force participation rate of African American women—which far surpassed that of white women—was judged by the dominant white, middle-income standard. Racial discrimination created an "other" with a different history.

The Work of African American Women

The gradual emancipation of black slaves during the eighteenth century in the northern colonies and the free African Americans that lived in the South created, in the early nineteenth century, a group of workers even more vulnerable than poor whites.[41] Freed black men became part of the chronically unemployed, "the strolling poor," along with freed (from bound apprenticeships), unskilled, white servants. Competition for work and the de-skilling of work characteristic of industrial wage labor, mixed with growing racial fear and discrimination among whites, resulted in limited access to skilled laboring positions for most black men. For them, the labor market consisted primarily in casual work.[42]

In the nineteenth-century antebellum North, African American workers were simply excluded from factory work, except for sweeping floors. They remained in the primarily unskilled, and frequently dangerous, labor that racism permitted: dock hands, carriage drivers, waiters, draymen, domestic servants, farmhands, seamen. Freed black women, in both North and South, worked primarily as servants, laundresses, and seamstresses.[43] Without legal protections or political voice, freed black workers were subject to abuses for which they had no defense. Some freed slaves bound themselves to their former masters in order to avoid an uncertain future in this labor market. Yet, even these minimal jobs were endangered when new immigrants struggled to gain access to wage labor.[44]

In the antebellum period of the nineteenth century, the economic role of slavery cannot be overemphasized. Slave-grown cotton was the leading export of the United States. It paid for the import of products and capital that fueled the national economy. According to David Brion Davis, the value of slaves in 1860 was three times the amount that had been invested in manufacturing or railroads nationwide.[45] Northerners shipped foodstuffs, timber, clothes, and shoes to slaveholders and consumed slave-produced rum, rice, cotton, tobacco, hemp, and other goods. The entire U.S. society was enmeshed in the economics of slavery.

Slaves existed to work. Everything slaves did, including the childbearing of African American women, contributed to their owner's economic well-being. Unable to marry legally, subject to separation from partners and children at any time, and ultimately owned by white masters, African American slaves created a sexual morality that supported marriage and stable unions when possible, did not stigmatize premarital sex, and welcomed the children even of coercive sexual unions.[46] Chattel slavery reveals without subtlety the abandonment of any pretense by white society to value black families and the willingness to skew gender identities, roles, and responsibilities in the service of capital accumulation.

Black women did all of the types of work considered domestic: cleaning, sewing, canning, cooking, personal services, and midwifery. They also did all the forms of manual labor associated with farming and men's work: planting, hoeing, harvesting, fixing equipment, mending fences, digging fence holes and ditches, and repairing roads. Similarly, in the antebellum southern experience of industrialization, employers who owned factories, mills, and forges put together a work force from whatever labor was locally available. Black slaves, either owned or leased, worked side by side with white wage earners in a manner that caused one observer to conclude that racial prejudice was not as strong in the South as it was in the North.[47] Children, women, and men worked in the same mill.

Owners debated the relative merits to capital accumulation of slave labor versus "free" wage labor. On the one hand, some argued that wage labor was good for the southern community because it provided a stake in society for landless poor, or "dirt poor," whites. Most textile mills employed poor, young, white, rural girls. For example, the mills in Graniteville, North Carolina, depended upon young daughters from the countryside whose parents camped out nearby creating mill villages. Company stores flourished as they monopolized the village and recaptured the wages of mill workers. Jones describes twelve-year-old girls working up to fourteen hours a day for an average wage of three dollars a week. On the other hand, despite these advantages in using wage labor, other manufacturers argued for the benefits of a more stable work force through slave labor. Slaves didn't walk off the job. Money spent in training them would be repaid by years of work. In down times, slaves could be put to other tasks, and leased slaves could be returned to owners. To these advantages of slavery, the supporters of wage labor countered that white workers could be fired and laid off without notice or financial responsibility for their subsistence. Racism finally settled the argument. As cotton growing boomed, increasing the need for slaves in the fields, factory owners turned more and more to white wage workers—a pattern of racial occupational segregation that would guide postbellum southern society as well.

In her book *More Than Chains and Toil,* Joan Martin contrasts the reality of slave work with the assumptions of the work-ethic ideal in white society. According to the white, middle-income ethic, all work is good. It enhances the development of moral character as well as advancing material well-being. The opportunity to engage in work that furthers one's goals in life is assumed to be open to everyone. Martin points out, however, that nothing in this work ethic acknowledges the reality of power relationships within society, relations of domination and subordination.[48] Yet that was the context of enslaved black women's lives. Their work supported white families within social institutions that denied the value of black families and gave no support to either their family or community ties.

But enslaved women also performed the labor that maintained the black family and community under such harsh conditions. Out of that lived experience, they developed their own work ethic. On the one hand, writes Martin, "Enslaved blackwomen knew fundamentally that work under forced labor and living was wrong." Work that was exploitive caused suffering and was evil. On the other hand, "In relation to resistance for self, family, and community in the midst of oppression, work was a source of faithful, moral living." Work that sustained the living and their relationships and resisted oppression was work that was meaningful and humanly fulfilling.[49]

Emancipation did little to improve the conditions of work for most African Americans. But it provided manufacturers and planters an army of free labor. In the postbellum South, where more than 90 percent of African Americans lived, black men in sharecropping families were subject now to the exploitation of work that was slavery except in name. Jones comments on the contradictory forces that sharecropping families faced. On the one hand, agricultural economic production and the desperate poverty of both freed black workers and sharecropping black families encouraged kin groups to remain close together. On the other hand, seasonal variations and the exploitive contracts of sharecropping made leaving one's family to find additional income necessary for survival.[50] Black women continued to do the same work after emancipation that they had done before: field work, household domestic service, and laundry work. Migration north did not change the circumstances of black labor. Angela Davis cites an 1899 study of black workers in Pennsylvania: 60 percent of all black workers were in some form of domestic service, and 91 percent of black women workers were employed as domestics.[51] According to the 1900 census only 5 percent of black women held higher-paid occupations.

North and South, the vulnerabilities embedded in "free" wage labor, multiplied by the pervasive impact of discrimination in all areas of life, led to desperate conditions for most African American families throughout the Jim Crow era. While white women activists deplored the idea of mothers' employment, the prevalence of married women's employment as a widespread necessity among African American families created a different perspective among black women activists. Women such as Fanny Jackson Coppin and Nannie Burroughs in the 1870s and, later, in the first half of the twentieth century, Mary Church Terrell, focused on the employment issues that impacted all but a small percent of the African American population: higher wages, better working conditions, and the establishment of kindergartens for the children of working mothers. As Linda Gordon writes: "Race issues were poverty issues, and women's issues were race issues. Race uplift work was usually welfare work by definition. . . ."[52] For that small percentage of African American women who achieved success in professional work around the turn of the century, high levels of individual achievement as social workers, librarians, nurses, and teachers were accompanied by "a sense of mutual obligation among the women, their families, and the larger black community."[53] The gendered, white work ethic of individualism was rejected by African American women and men for a work ethic of personal improvement that was committed to the survival and development of the entire community.

Yet, in a theme now quite familiar, public guardians of respectability pronounced the families of free blacks at fault for their destitution. John Calhoun in 1844 cited the natural lack of family virtues in freed northern blacks as the cause of vice, poverty, and insanity. Without natural virtues, blacks were said to need the paternalism of the slave system. Similarly, Robert Toombs, a former senator, observed in the 1870s that "the negro" knows nothing of marriage responsibilities, no more than a farm animal. According to Toombs, natural black immorality and animal instincts had been released from the external control that slavery had provided.[54]

By the early 1920s, the theme was played to a different tune. This time white knowledge-producers argued that slavery itself had been responsible for destroying the orders of nature once present in the black family.[55] In reality, the forms of black families after emancipation were not so dissimilar from those of white families despite their exclusion from skilled and factory work, despite poverty and unemployment, and despite hazardous work and unsanitary urban slums. As the deep recession of the late nine-teenth century created even fewer good earning opportunities for black men, some African American households responded by splitting up in the pursuit of work. Others responded by adding nonfamily members to a household that included both parents. And the higher mortality rates of black men caused by dangerous jobs increased the black rate of marital dissolution due to death.[56]

Organic Connections

Renditions of history that do not pay attention to differences of gender, race, and class often begin with the assumption that current beliefs and practices are "natural." That is, these historical accounts assume that things were always the way they are, or that they inevitably developed this way. Or it is assumed that the way things developed was the best of any possible alternative. White Americans, especially, seem to assume that history is, after all, progress. Telling "history" in this framework is then a matter of, first, identifying the practices, events, and persons who supported the strand of development that triumphed and, second, of ignoring the exis-tence of alternative views and practices. What is forgotten is that "what happened" was produced out of social conflict; and that this conflict, at the same time, constructed persons, institutions, and belief systems.

Industrialization did not simply move the making of market products from the home to the factory. It did not simply reduce the household to a unit of consumption. As the primary vehicle for the expansion of capital-ism's wage system of labor, the vast changes in the political economy encompassed by the term "industrialization" overthrew the means by which most white men understood and lived out the social responsibilities of their gender. Most white men found themselves in the chaos of new eco-nomic insecurity over which they had no control: business cycles, depen-dence on cash income, decreasing wages, and loss of traditional skills. They lost much of their status as fathers who had performed the generational work of preparing sons for manhood by passing down the skills and tools of their trade. And in the new social relations established by wage work in a capitalist system, they lost community status as that status shifted from valuing men who worked hard and productively to valuing men who were successful in capital accumulation.[57]

It is in response to this chaos that the ideology of differentiated gender spheres was reshaped and the erasure of women's work from social aware-ness made sense. Masculinizing wage work preserved white men's privileged access to cash income, despite the instability of that access for many. As only wage work became valued as work, "economy" (literally, the management of the household) was divorced from domestic activities. The restructuring of gender and race relations maintained white male privilege on new terms in the transition from an agrarian society to a society restructured on wage labor and contractual relationships. In the process, according to Eisenstein, "The economic and social position of most women declined. . . ."[58] By maintaining male control over property, wages, and inheritance, industrial capitalism changed work, family forms, and gender definitions. It changed the sex/gender system. But it maintained male domination over women and children, white male domination over people of color; and it established the domination of the white male owners of capital over everyone.[59]

At the same time, the restructuring of gender and different structuring of race served the logic of capital accumulation. Capitalism is a system in which capital-as-money, wealth, must be extracted from the process of producing goods and services in order to finance growth; that is, the extraction of more wealth in an ever-repeated process.[60] Racial and gendered ideologies functioned to ease this process by which wealth is "systematically channeled from the broad working body of society into the hands of a restricted group or class" for the specific purpose of using that wealth to repeat the process in order to extract more wealth.[61] Capitalism, then, is the web of social relations, distinguished in the United States by race, gender, and class relations, that makes this accumulation process possible.

First, men were encouraged to accept wage work. In exchange, wage work, the primary source of money, gendered as masculine, provided a new basis for masculine identity. This would be the new masculine activity by which men provided for their families and, in that way, contributed to their communities. Wage work, ideologically, was made a male privilege, specifically a white male privilege.

Once the satisfaction of masculine responsibilities was centered on wage work, social relations among white men could be realigned to serve capital accumulation. The work of creating profit could now be interpreted as a social responsibility that in and of itself contributed to the social good. It was rewarded with social status and personal wealth. Unlike the pre-industrial agrarian economy, the wage system required no sense of relationship beyond the contractual agreement. Relations between free men, the well-to-do employer and the desperately poor laborer, were purely contractual. Calculations of economic rationality, defined by legal

contract and based on an ideology of masculine autonomy, reshaped relationships of productive work and reestablished the basis for social status.

The merging of masculine privilege with wage work, and the erasure of
women's activities from economic sight, also permitted the payment of
inadequate wages, thus facilitating the further accumulation of wealth at a
time when that was particularly difficult, yet essential, for the expansion of
early capitalism. Boydston estimates that among the poorest of households
in the mid-nineteenth century, a wife's nonpaid labor added "roughly $250
a year beyond maintenance." The value added by the work of middle-
income wives was comparable even if only typical housework activities are
counted and even if the cost of servants is subtracted. However, few
women could actually earn this much in wage work. Consequently the economic value of wives was embedded in the family unit and invisible to a
society in which social status was focused on male wages. Marriage actually increased the economic well-being of working-class men as well as
middle-income men by adding a worker whose unpaid domestic labor
sustained the home and freed the husband to pursue wage work. Boydston
concludes:

> Employers were enabled by the presence of this sizeable but uncounted
> labor in the home to pay both men and women wages that were, in fact,
> below the level of subsistence. The difference was critical to the develop-
> ment of industrialization in the antebellum Northeast.[62]

Finally, the logic of the wage system in a free (that is, contractual) labor
market assumed that a wage accepted is an adequate wage according to the
market's impartial measure. When workers are paid (presumably) according to the value of their work to the market, their poverty, wives who work,
and children who are street urchins cannot be blamed on the inadequacy
of wages. Rather, the poverty of immigrants, of the white working class,
and of people of color in the nineteenth century can be explained as "a sign
of indolence and savagery" while "wealth symbolized the expenditure of
labor toward the betterment of society."[63] In the common sense of capitalist logic, enhanced by scientific definitions of race and the development of
Social Darwinism, a free labor market severed the moral connection
between wealth and poverty. Cloth, shoes, hats, household tools, and other
manufactured goods became affordable for those families in which a father
worked hard for his middle-income (also generally inadequate) wages and
a good mother stayed at home to raise children in conformity with the values that would, in turn, make them good workers and good citizens.

But, as Stephanie Coontz summarizes,

> For every nineteenth-century middle-class family that protected its wife and child within the family circle, then, there was an Irish or a German girl scrubbing floors in that middle-class home, a Welsh boy mining coal to keep home-baked goodies warm, a black girl doing the family laundry, a black mother and child picking cotton to be made into clothes for the family, and a Jewish or an Italian daughter in a sweatshop making "ladies" dresses or artificial flowers for the family to purchase.[64]

"Good" families depended on the work of those women, men, and children who by their working revealed themselves, according to middle-income sensibilities, to be the cause of their own misfortune. By this paradox, affluent white Christian families maintained their family values (a new sex/gender system integrated into industrial capitalism) by purchasing the material standard of living these values required from others' families whose wages were inadequate to reach these middle-income Christian standards.[65] The cost of "ideal" families rests on the survival strategies that make other families deviant. In this way, ideals function to legitimate benefits derived from exploitive race and class relationships.

WOMEN AND WORK TODAY

The partnership between industrial capitalism and patriarchy constructed "family" and "work" as ideal opposites: opposites spacially, opposites in gender, and opposites in the types of values and character appropriate to each space. The partnership constructed a society and its various institutions to reflect that ideology. In doing so, it rendered invisible or perverse the work of most women whose lives revealed the actual interrelatedness and interdependence of family work and market work.

Most U.S. families did not achieve the middle- and upper-income ideal until after the Second World War. Then, for a short period in the 1950s, a majority of U.S. families for the first time finally achieved the nineteenth-century nuclear-family ideal: a middle-income life supported by the wages of a husband and the unpaid family work of a stay-at-home wife.[66] Those of us who remember with some nostalgia this golden age of the family typically fail to remember two aspects of this unique decade.[67]

First, we fail to remember the role of the political economy in supporting stable family well-being for some families. At that time, about 40 percent of young men were eligible for veterans' benefits, which included most of the tuition for college education. Almost 20 percent of government expenditures in 1950 were for public works: new schools, water and sewage, interstate highways. The government underwrote down payments and long-term mortgages for those who had been turned away by mortgage companies. Thousands of young men trained for good careers through the National Education Defense Act.

Where did the money come from? Much came from corporate taxation—about 23 percent in the 1950s. Meanwhile, workers were gaining more return from their work. The '50s saw the median paycheck more than double, with the greatest gains made by the lowest 20 percent. Historian Kenneth Jackson argues that this was the first period in the history of the world that the pattern of wealth distribution was neither pyramidal nor the reverse.[68] Workers worked a shorter week and had less to worry about from layoffs or plant closings. When Levittown opened, a factory worker could earn the closing costs needed in one day of work. By 1991 that factory worker would need to work eighteen weeks.[69]

But these blessings were not enjoyed by all—and that is the second thing we sometimes do not remember. This utopia for some rested on pervasive discrimination against others: women; racial, ethnic, and political minorities; Jews; gays and lesbians. At the end of the 1950s, about 20 percent of U.S. children lived below the poverty line—as did almost half of African American married families. The FHA deemed homes in neighborhoods where blacks lived to be risky investments. They were "red-lined."[70] The isolation of African American poor and rural poor from newly suburban middle-income white families made invisible those excluded from the political and economic supports of this political economy. They were what Michael Harrington later called "The Other America."[71] Nonetheless, the image of the 1950s family has become a misleading symbol for the way families used to be, and, for some, the way they ought to be. It continues to mask the differences created by race, class, and gender.

Today, just a brief fifty years later, the short-lived social compact created between white male workers, corporations, and government during and after World War II has been severely eroded. Families with children in which both parents go off to work constitute a majority (51 percent) of all married-couple families.[72] In 1999, both parents were employed full-time in a little less than 40 percent of all two-parent families with school-age children.[73] Single parents (almost all of whom are mothers) and dual-earner families are the most common types of families represented in the work force today.[74] Of those parents with a child under eighteen in their household, today's work force includes 96 percent of fathers, 68 percent of married mothers, 74 percent of once-married mothers, and over 50 percent of never-married mothers.[75] While the dramatic influx of women, particularly married white mothers, into the wage labor force is often interpreted as a significant victory for the feminist movement, the material story behind the veneer of greater gender equality and U.S. prosperity in the 1980s and 1990s is quite different.

Between 1979 and 1995, real hourly wages (that is, wages adjusted for changes in the cost of living) fell for the bottom 70 percent of wage earners.[76] Real wages fell for most American men. Over the period from 1989 to 1997, the bottom 80 percent of American male workers continued to experience the decrease in real wages that had begun at the end of the 1970s.[77] For the 80 percent of the work force that are production and non-supervisory workers, real hourly wages were lower in 1999 than in 1979.[78] In fact, from 1979 to 1995 (after which wages began to rise) the wage decline for the median male worker amounted to about 15 percent.[79] The decline was greatest among young workers and workers without a college degree (who are three-fourths of the work force). Yet family incomes have grown slightly during this period, although at historically slow rates. Carnoy explains why:

> The U.S. average real wage (corrected for changes in the cost of living) fell (for men and women combined) 9.7 percent between 1975 and 1995, and the median income for all males with income fell 8.2 percent. Median real income for families, however, rose 9.2 percent during the same period. This suggests that married women, working at lower wages than men, more than made up for the difference in family income by working more hours, on average, than in 1975.[80]

The traditional family—that is, the white, middle-income nuclear family—has become the nontraditional, dual-earner family, as an economic survival strategy in the face of the retreat of business and government from supporting the family. Whereas the *unpaid* labor of middle-income wives was essential for a middle-income standard of living for families in the nineteenth century, today the *paid* labor of wives and mothers has become essential for most middle-income families.[81] This change is part of the larger transformation of the U.S. economy from an industrial economy to a postindustrial one in which manufacturing jobs are lost as service-sector jobs multiply.

Today, the entrance of middle-income (especially white) women into the wage labor force serves the needs of capital accumulation in two ways.

First, women provide cheaper labor than men both in the sense of receiving unequal pay for the same work and in the sense of being clustered into occupations designated as female occupations.[82] Of all women who work for wages, 75 percent are in just twenty occupations, each of which is 80 percent or more female. Studies have also shown a strong statistical relationship between wage levels and the concentration of women in a given occupation. Wages decline as the percentage of women in the occupation increases.[83] Where women have entered predominately male fields, they tend to be clustered at the bottom of the wage/prestige continuum. For example, while women comprise 26 percent of all lawyers, they are only 2 percent of the partners in major law firms. Even when accounting for occupational or for educational differences, women's weekly earnings average about three-fourths of men's.

This phenomenon of segregation and wage inequality is global. Everywhere women are entering the formal work force, contributing significantly to the income of families, and are often the sole supporters of their families. Yet, in both the overdeveloped and the two-thirds world, controlling for the type of work, women earn about 75 percent or less of what men earn.[84]

Second, in the United States, all of the net increase in job creation in the last two decades has been in the service sector, where average wages are low and have declined in real terms.[85] Women are disproportionately employed in service-sector occupations, making up two-thirds of service workers. And much service work is work that is traditionally associated with the caregiving of women: food preparation and service (cooks and waitresses), cleaning and building services (maids, janitors, and elevator operators), health services (nurses' aides, dental assistants, orderlies), and personal services (hairdressers, barbers, childcare workers).[86] For example, women make up 86.3 percent of all the low-prestige, low-pay health service workers. They are almost 90 percent of table servers. Clerical work, once a male-dominated occupation, is now almost exclusively a female occupation. Women comprise 90 percent of bank tellers, 97 percent of receptionists, 99 percent of secretaries.[87] In the new economy, the employment of women in lower paying service work is crucial to the process of capital accumulation.

Race, as always, makes a difference. African American families have historically employed the strategy of using more employed workers to support the family, even when working mothers were judged by affluent white women and men as bad mothers creating dysfunctional families. Thus, the labor force participation rates of black and white women during the twentieth century follow different patterns. Black women's participation rate remains relatively constant, around 40 percent, from 1900 to mid-century, before climbing sharply from 1950 to 1990, when it reached almost 60 percent. White women's participation rate rose steadily, but slowly, from 1900 to 1950. From 1950 it climbed steeply, reaching over 50 percent by 1990 when the gap in the labor force participation rates of black and white women almost closed (59.5 percent and 56.4 percent, respectively).[88] In 2000, black women's labor force participation rate continued to exceed that of white women: 63.2 percent and 59.8 percent.[89]

Moreover, the intersection of gender, race, and class makes the experience of work and its benefits quite different for different groups of women workers. Throughout the first half of the century, black women earned income through the only jobs open to them: agricultural work and private domestic service. These were also the occupations exempted from the social insurance programs created in the 1930s. The result was that most black workers, men and women, were ineligible for the social reforms of the New Deal: unemployment benefits, workers' compensation, and social security benefits. Thus, when in 1963 Betty Friedan proclaimed that "work can now be seen as the key to the problem that has no name," Paula Giddings's response, that this view "seemed to come from another planet," reflected a long and different experience of employment than that envisioned by the wives of white men.[90]

It should be no surprise then that the increased economic instability of most families since the late 1970s, noted in aggregate terms above, hit the families of people of color differently and disproportionately. While always concentrated in lower paying occupations, black workers began to be replaced by even lower-wage labor in the 1970s: particularly by new immigrants from Latin America and Asia. Plant closings, especially in the steel and automobile industries, and the movement of retail and clerical work into suburbs that were predominantly white and rural areas contributed to black unemployment rates averaging 15.2 percent between 1975 and 1986, compared to a rate of less than 7 percent for European Americans.[91] By 1990, 30 percent of black women workers were employed in primary-sector jobs, (that is, "good" jobs), compared to 40 percent of white women workers. However, the vast majority of black professional women and technical workers, and half of black female managers are in government or private nonprofit-sector employment. Consequently these women are disproportionately subject to lower wages or the uncertainties of political budget debates.[92]

Similarly, while clerical work, service work, and sales provided white women a step up from factory work, for women of color it has provided only a "move over" from domestic work to other forms of lowest-skill, lowest-wage work.[93] For black women, service work is more likely to be the most menial of work and is more likely to be a permanent job category.[94] Consequently, the disparity in wages between white women workers and black women workers, which had almost disappeared in the late 1970s, has grown larger through the 1980s and 1990s. Andolsen reports that in 1996, black women who worked full time and year round earned eighty-five cents in comparison to each dollar earned by white women.[95]

The point, of course, is that the new, white, middle-income survival strategy of adding the wife and mother to the work force in response to increasingly harsh economic conditions is a strategy that has long been in use by black families. But the success of this strategy is connected to the larger context of the role of race and gender in organizing employed work. Using 1988 data, Oliver and Shapiro describe the difference in results:

> Among married couples it takes two full-time workers in 60 percent of black homes to earn between $25,000 and $50,000 yearly; the same is true for only 37 percent of white homes. Among all married couples with a middle-income standard of living, both spouses worked at least some time in the paid labor force in 78 percent of black families and in 62 percent of white families.[96]

For most families only time spent in paid employment has any impact on family income.[97] To make up for significant wage differentials, black families must not only add workers but must also add hours simply not to lose ground. Thus, while most families are working more, the growth in hours worked is greater in families of color. But, as we have seen, a dual-earner survival strategy does not achieve similar results across racial lines. Mishel provides a striking comparison:

> ... in 1998, the average middle-income, married-couple African American family with children worked 489 more hours per year than a comparable white family in the same income range. That is, the middle-income black family worked 12 more weeks than the average white family in order to reach the middle-income ranks.[98]

History reveals that the organization of all the work that is necessary for human survival is a result of the power relations embedded within existing institutions of society. For ethicists, it is a question of social justice. In the United States the means of amassing capital have been interlocked with gender and race relations, shaping family forms as it shapes families' differing options for survival. However, throughout this history the family norm of middle- and upper-class white Americans has functioned to establish the social ideals by which other families are found lacking, even as these ideals themselves shift under the demands of new economic practices. Today families with different options face growing isolation and distress as the fabric of community support once available to some is further unraveled by neoliberal policies. In the face of this reality, talk of family values that bemoans the presumed inadequacy of families struggling to survive these policies reveals only the arrogance of privilege.

NOTES

1. W. E. B. DuBois, quoted in Manning Marable, *Blackwater: Historical Studies in Race, Class Consciousness, and Revolution* (Niwot, Colo.: University Press of Colorado, 1981; rev. ed. 1993), 69.

2. In 1960 the rate of participation of women in the labor force, including both married and single women, was about 35 percent (compared to about 15 percent in 1900 and 23 percent in 1950). About 31 percent of white, married women were in the labor force in 1960. Social science research and general public opinion assumed that the employment of mothers had ill effects on the development of children. It was not until the early 1980s that reviews of existing empirical studies began to cast doubt on the simple cause-and-effect conclusions that had been made. 1980 appears to be the tipping point: that time at which the employment of wives in married-couple families became the numerical standard. Teresa Amott and Julie Matthaei, *Race, Gender, and Work: A Multi-Cultural Economic History of Women in the United States,* rev. ed. (Boston: South End Press, 1996), 305; Claudia Goldin, *Understanding the Gender Gap: An Economic History of American Women* (New York: Oxford University Press, 1990), 119–20; Sharlene Hesse-Biber and Gregg Lee Carter, *Working Women in America: Split Dreams* (New York: Oxford University Press, 2000), 7; Karla B. Hackstaff, *Marriage in a Culture of Divorce* (Philadelphia: Temple University Press, 1999), 231 n. 1.

3. Betty Friedan, *The Feminine Mystique* (1963; reprint, with introduction and epilogue, New York: Laurel, 1983), 32.

4. Ibid., ix.

5. The term "work" used in an unqualified way refers to the activities of producing products and services for private or market consumption *and* to the activities of reproducing the human generations and caring for their dependent members. Where this full sense is not intended, I use qualifying terms such as "wage work" or "reproductive work."

6. *The State of the World's Women 1985* (Oxford: New Internationalist Publications, 1985), 3.

7. Jeanne Boydston, *Home and Work: Housework, Wages, and the Ideology of Labor in the Early Republic* (New York: Oxford University Press, 1990). See "Introduction."

8. Stephanie Coontz, *The Social Origins of Private Life: A History of American Families 1600–1900* (New York: Verso, 1988), 83. The sociological term is, typically, "nuclear-augmented."

9. Ibid., 162–63.

10. Boydston, *Home and Work,* 18.

11. Coontz, *Social Origins,* 97–98. This explanation of women's subordination reflects the teachings of John Calvin. See Lisa Sowle Cahill, *Family: A Christian Social Perspective* (Minneapolis: Fortress Press, 2000).

12. Steven Mintz and Susan Kellogg, *Domestic Revolutions: A Social History of American Family Life* (New York: Free Press, 1988), 49–50.

13. Boydston, *Home and Work,* 28

14. Ibid., 9. Italics included in the original.

15. Julie Matthaei, *An Economic History of Women in America: Women's Work, the Sexual Division of Labor, and the Development of Capitalism* (New York: Schocker Books, 1982), 33–34.

16. Boydston, *Home and Work,* xviii.

17. Catherine Beecher, cited in Mintz and Kellogg, *Domestic Revolutions,* 57.

18. Boydston, *Home and Work,* 102–7.

19. Ibid., 162–63.

20. Jesse T. Peck, *The True Woman; or, Life and Happiness at Home and Abroad* (New York: Carlton and Porter, 1857), 242–44, cited in Boydston, *Home and Work,* 144, 146.

21. The use of the term "gentile" is also striking here for several reasons. White American Christians, claiming themselves and their nation as the new "chosen" people, appropriate usage of the Jewish term "gentile" to indicate their own chosenness in opposition to all others. In addition, the arena of productive, market-oriented work is denounced as outside the space of holiness—the home.

22. Carroll Smith-Rosenberg, *Disorderly Conduct: Visions of Gender in Victorian America* (New York: Alfred A. Knopf, 1985), 197–216.

23. Tamara K. Hareven, *Family Time and Industrial Time: The Relationship between the Family and Work in a New England Industrial Community* (Cambridge: Cambridge University Press, 1982), 83.

24. Sean Wilentz, *Chants Democratic: New York City and the Rise of the American Working Class, 1788–1850* (New York: Oxford University Press, 1984), 117, 405 Table 14), cited in Boydston, *Home and Work,* 58–62.

25. Coontz, *Social Origins,* 167.

26. Hareven, *Family Time and Industrial Time,* 259. Subsequent data is taken from chap. 10, "Career Advancement."

27. Howard Zinn, *A People's History of the United States, 1492–Present*, rev. ed. (New York: Harper Perennial, 1995), 218.

28. Amott and Matthaei, *Race, Gender, and Work*, 100–101.

29. Zinn, *A People's History of the United States*, 216.

30. John D'Emilio and Estelle B. Freedman, *Intimate Matters: A History of Sexuality in America* (New York: Harper & Row, 1988), 131.

31. Jacqueline Jones, *American Work: Four Centuries of Black and White Labor* (New York: W. W. Norton, 1998), 156–62. To deal with growing numbers of the poor, as early as the beginning of the eighteenth century, various cities experimented with workhouses. These were large buildings where many people, primarily widows (or wives whose husbands had disappeared) and their children, were closely supervised, highly restricted, and paid too little to live on as they performed textile-related work: carding wool and spinning wool and flax. The "bettering house" in Philadelphia combined the poor, vagrants, and criminals together for punishment and rehabilitation. It closed its doors after the Revolution for failure to earn its subscribers a profit.

32. Goldin, *Understanding the Gender Gap*, 50.

33. Hareven, *Family Time and Industrial Time*, 4.

34. Ibid., 78.

35. Ibid., 366.

36. As Johanna Brenner points out, there is always a material basis for beliefs. This sexual division of labor had material support in the reality of women's role in childbirth and breastfeeding, in working-class families' need for larger families, in the real labor that domestic work involved, and in the lack of social supports within productive work that would have enabled mothers to participate: on-site care for infants, nursing breaks for working mothers, paid maternity leave, and so forth. Thus, working-class families supported efforts to gain a "family wage." See Johanna Brenner, *Women and the Politics of Class* (New York: Monthly Review Press, 2000), 27–36.

37. Linda Gordon, *Pitied But Not Entitled: Single Mothers and the History of Welfare, 1890–1935* (New York: Free Press, 1994), 31, 135.

38. Matthaei, *An Economic History*, 33–34.

39. See Goldin, *Understanding the Gender Gap*, chap. 6.

40. Christine Bose, "Devaluing Women's Work: The Undercount of Women's Employment in 1900 and 1980," in *Hidden Aspects of Women's Work*, ed. Christine Bose, Roslyn Feldberg, and Natalie Sokoloff (New York: Praeger, 1987), 98.

41. In 1790 the first national census reported that 8 percent of African Americans were free. Amott and Matthaei, *Race, Gender, and Work*, 149.

42. Jones, *American Work*, 162–66.

43. Amott and Matthaei, *Race, Gender, and Work*, 150.

44. Jones, *American Work*, 282–86.

45. David Brion Davis, "The Enduring Legacy of the South's Civil War Victory," *New York Times*, 26 August 2001: WK 1, WK 6. Davis argues that chattel slavery

was essential to early U.S. capital accumulation. New England merchants shipped supplies needed by slaves to the South and to the West Indies. Northerners and Europeans consumed the sugar, rum, cotton, tobacco, indigo, and hemp grown by slaves. Eighteenth-century contemporaries in French Canada attributed the economic success of the English colonies to African slave labor and requested permission to import their own slaves.

46. D'Emilio and Freedman, *Intimate Matters*, 97.

47. Jones, *American Work*, 224. This discussion of southern industrialization is taken from Jones, chap. 7, "The Racial Politics of Southern Labor."

48. Joan Martin, *More Than Chains and Toil: A Christian Work Ethic of Enslaved Women* (Louisville, Ky.: Westminster John Knox Press, 2000), 133–38.

49. Ibid., 105–9.

50. Jacqueline Jones, *The Dispossessed: America's Underclasses from the Civil War to the Present* (New York: Basic Books, 1992), 37.

51. Angela Davis, *Women, Race, and Class* (New York: Vintage, 1983), 93, 98. As late as 1960 most employed African American women worked in private domestic or nondomestic service jobs.

52. Linda Gordon, *Pitied But Not Entitled*, 132. For her discussion of black maternal feminists, see chap. 5.

53. Stephanie J. Shaw, *What a Woman Ought to Be and to Do: Black Professional Women Workers During the Jim Crow Era* (Chicago: University of Chicago Press, 1996), 2.

54. Stephanie Coontz, *The Way We Never Were: American Families and the Nostalgia Trap* (New York: Basic Books, 1992), 235–36.

55. Ibid., 236–37.

56. Ibid., 237–43.

57. Spokesmen in the current men's movement also make note of these attacks on men's sense of masculinity and the negative impact of wage work away from the family on men's relationships with their sons. See Robert Bly, *Iron John: A Book about Men* (New York: Vintage Books, 1990); and Sam Keen, *Fire in the Belly: On Being a Man* (New York: Bantam Books, 1991).

58. Zillah Eisenstein, *The Radical Future of Liberal Feminism* (Boston: Northeastern University Press,1981), 98.

59. Drawing on the work of Gayle Rubin, Nancy Chodorow defines the "sex/gender system" as "a fundamental determining and constituting element of that society, socially constructed, subject to historical change and development, and organized in such a way that it is systematically reproduced" (Nancy Chodorow, *The Reproduction of Mothering: Psychoanalysis and the Sociology of Gender* [Berkeley: University of California Press, 1978], 8). It is "a set of arrangements by which the biological raw material of human sex and procreation is shaped by human, social intervention and satisfied in a conventional manner . . ." (Rubin, "The Traffic in Women: Notes on the 'Political Economy' of Sex," in *Toward an Anthropology of Women*, ed. Reyna Reiter [New York: Monthly Review Press, 1975], 165–66).

60. The concept of economic growth plays an essential role in capitalism's ideological promise of equal opportunity. Michael Novak argues that democracy itself depends upon "the reality" of economic growth. He writes: "no fair and free system can possibly guarantee equal outcomes. A democratic system depends for its legitimacy, therefore, not upon equal results but upon a sense of equal opportunity. Such legitimacy flows from the belief of all individuals that they can better their condition. This belief can be realized only under the conditions of economic growth" (Novak, *The Spirit of Democratic Capitalism* [Lanham, Md.: Madison Books, 1982, 1991], 15).

61. Robert L. Heilbroner, *The Nature and Logic of Capitalism* (New York: W. W. Norton, 1985), 33–38.

62. Boydston, *Home and Work*, 132–39.

63. Mrs. Jane Marcet, *Conversations on Political Economy; in which the Elements of that Science are Familiarly Explained*, 7th ed. (London: Longman, Orme, Brown, Green, & Longmans, 1839), 25–72, cited in Boydston, *Home and Work*, 160.

64. Coontz, *The Way We Never Were*, 11–12.

65. Statistically, the United States was in the nineteenth century, as it is today, predominantly Christian in religious affiliation.

66. Coontz, *The Way We Never Were*, 24.

67. Coontz, *The Way We Really Are: Coming to Terms with America's Changing Families* (New York: Basic Books, 1997), chap. 2, "What We Really Miss About the 1950's."

68. Kenneth Jackson, *Crabgrass Frontier: The Suburbanization of the United States* (New York: Oxford University Press, 1985), 290f.

69. Coontz, *The Way We Really Are*, 41–43.

70. Ibid., 43–44.

71. Michael Harrington, *The Other America* (New York: Macmillan, 1962).

72. National Council on Family Relations, *Public Policy Through a Family Lens: Sustaining Families in the 21st Century* (Minneapolis: National Council on Family Relations, 2000), 6. The NCFR publishes two journals, *Journal of Marriage and Family* and *Family Relations*.

73. Steve Hipple of the Bureau of Labor Statistics, cited in Ann Crittenden, *The Price of Motherhood: Why the Most Important Job in the World Is Still the Least Valued* (New York: Metropolitan Books, 2001), 277 n. 8.

74. Eileen Drake, "A Legal Perspective on Work-Family Issues," in *Integrating Work and Family: Challenges and Choices for a Changing World*, ed. Saroj Parasuraman and Jeffrey H. Greenhaus (Westport, Conn.: Quorum Books, 1997), 123.

75. U.S. Department of Labor, Women's Bureau, *Women Workers: Trends and Issues* (Washington, D.C.: Department of Labor, 1994), 1, 11. Also James A. Levine and Todd L. Pittinsky, *Working Fathers: New Strategies for Balancing Work and Family* (Reading, Mass.: Addison-Wesley, 1997), 9.

76. Lawrence Mishel, Jared Bernstein, and John Schmitt, *The State of Working America 2000–2001* (Ithaca, N.Y.: Cornell University Press, 2001), 123. However,

wage trends are only part of this story of more time in wage work and less reward. Reduced and lost benefits are another part. The share of the work force that is covered by employer-sponsored health benefits has declined from 70 percent in 1979 to about 63 percent in 1998. In 1991 most of these were in traditional fee-for-service plans; by 1997 almost three-fourths of covered employees were in HMOs. Employee contributions for health care coverage and co-payments have risen. Dental coverage has almost disappeared. However, high premiums and tight restrictions, such as long waiting periods before enrollment, keep many workers without coverage even when working for companies that offer health insurance plans. Low-wage earners are the hardest hit. The retail sector has the lowest rate of insured employees. While this is partly because of its high percentage of part-time employees, it is also because of its high average monthly employee contribution of $46 for premiums, compared to an average of $29 among all industries surveyed. Jennifer Steinhauer, "Hidden Barriers to Health Coverage," *New York Times*, 19 August 2001: BU 11. The trend in pensions is similar. See chap. 4.

77. Lawrence Mishel, Jared Bernstein, and John Schmitt, *The State of Working America 1998–1999* (Ithaca, N.Y.: Cornell University Press, 1999), 122–23.

78. Mishel et al., *2000–2001*, 121. Production and nonsupervisory workers include factory, construction, and a wide range of service-sector workers (but not higher-paid managers and supervisors). Average hourly earnings in 1979 were $13.87 and in 1999 they were $13.24. This general statement masks a turn upward in wages between 1995 and 1999 driven by low unemployment rates, an increase in the minimum wage, and faster productivity growth. Whether this more positive trend will continue and lead to new gains in real wages will depend upon what happens to these three factors.

79. Ibid., 125.

80. Martin Carnoy, *Sustaining the New Economy: Work, Family, and Community in the Information Age* (New York: Russell Sage, 2000), 136.

81. Explanations for the increase in women's labor force participation rate fall into two general categories. "Demand-side" explanations emphasize: (a) an increase in women's "human capital" making them more desirable workers; (b) a general rise in the demand for labor as the demand for goods and services increases; and (c) a rise in the demand for labor in specific sectors of the economy such as clerical and service work, which are female occupations. Supply-side explanations note: (a) rising wages for women because of an increase in demand for their labor; (b) demographic changes toward smaller families and more single women, including rising divorce rates; and (c) falling real wages for men. Joyce P. Jacobsen, *The Economics of Gender* (Cambridge, Mass.: Blackwell, 1994), 127.

82. Randy Albelda, Robert Drago, and Steven Shulman, *Unlevel Playing Fields: Understanding Wage Inequality and Discrimination* (New York: McGraw-Hill, 1997), chap. 2; U.S. Department of Labor, Women's Bureau, *1993 Handbook on Women Workers: Trends and Issues* (Washington, D.C.: Department of Labor,

1994), 34; Tamar Lewin, "Women Profit Less than Men in the Nonprofit World, Too," *New York Times*, 3 June 2001: Y23.

83. Hesse-Biber and Carter, *Working Women in America*, 54–56.

84. Ibid., 57–62.

85. James K. Galbraith, *Created Unequal: The Crisis in American Pay* (New York: Free Press, 1998), 155. The Bureau of Labor Statistics estimates that between 1998 and 2006 more than 95 percent of all work created will be in the service industries. "Bureau of Labor Statistics Releases New 1996–2006 Employment Projections" at www.bls.gov/news.release/ecopro.nws.htm.

86. Amott and Matthaei, *Race, Gender, and Work*, 328.

87. Hesse-Biber and Carter, *Working Women in America*, 129, 132, 117.

88. Amott and Matthaei, *Race, Gender, and Work*, 306–7. The participation rate in 1990 for married black women was still about 10 percent higher than that of married white women.

89. Bureau of Labor Statistics, "Civilian Labor Force 2000: Total 16 Years and Older," available at http://ftp.bls.gov/pub/special.requests/ep/labor.force/mlrtab 2000-03.txt.

90. Paula Giddings, *When and Where I Enter: The Impact of Black Women on Race and Sex in America* (New York: Bantam Books, 1984), 299.

91. Ibid., 179–80.

92. Ibid., 187.

93. Bette Woody, "Black Women in the New Services Economy: Help or Hindrance in Economic Self-Sufficiency?" (Wellesley, Mass.: Wellesley College Center for Research on Women, 1989), 54 (report available to order from www.wcwonline.org).

94. Marilyn Power and Sam Rosenberg, "Race, Class, and Occupational Mobility: Black and White Women in Service Work in the United States," in *Gender and Political Economy: Incorporating Diversity into Theory and Policy*, ed. Ellen Mutari, Heather Boushey, and William Fraher (Armonk, N.Y.: M. E. Sharpe, 1997), 150–69; Amott and Matthaei, *Race, Gender, and Work*, 328; Barbara Hilkert Andolsen, *The New Job Contract: Economic Justice in an Age of Insecurity* (Cleveland: Pilgrim Press, 1998), 68–71.

95. Ibid., 69. Another reason for this wage disparity is that the wage gap between college-educated women and low-wage women, in general, has increased significantly. Between 1989 and 1995 the real wages of the lowest 60 percent of women workers declined while the real wages of the top 20 percent of women workers increased.

96. Melvin L. Oliver and Thomas M. Shapiro, *Black Wealth/White Wealth: A New Perspective on Racial Inequality* (New York: Routledge, 1995), 96.

97. Randy Albelda and Chris Tilly, *Glass Ceilings and Bottomless Pits: Women's Work, Women's Poverty* (Boston: South End Press, 1997), 38–39. That is, most families depend on earned income as opposed to income from owning property or financial assets.

98. Mishel et al., *2000–2001*, 34.

3

The Cost of Kids

And as far as child care, the only person who really did take care of our daughter was her grandmother. And then health problems sort of arose with my mom, so she couldn't babysit for us. So that had an impact as far as on our income with my wife . . . she had to give up her job, so she could stay home with our daughter. 'Cause she really didn't want as far as any person taking care of our children. So that gave up her job and her salary and for her to stay home and to provide for our children and stay home and babysit and stuff like that. . . . . It is a big impact when you, you know, bring in two salaries, then all of a sudden one person stops working their job just to stay home and babysit.[1]

No current issue issue reveals the terms of the agreement reached between Western patriarchy and liberal capitalism in the nineteenth century as clearly as the issue of caring for children and, more generally, caring for dependent persons. In the women's suffrage campaign of the last century middle-income women were taunted with the question, "Who will care for the children when the women go off to vote?" Now, with the influx of most women into the wage-labor force, the crisis once limited to the families of the working poor is visited upon all families.

In 1999, about 40 percent of mothers in married couple families with children under the age of six worked full-time; another 20 percent worked part-time. About 38 percent were not counted as part of the formal labor force. Only 23 percent of all types of families with children younger than age six had one parent in wage work and one who stayed at home.[2] Most astonishing, 58 percent of all women with infants under one year of age were in the labor force.[3] Moreover, two recent studies have documented the rate of women's return to work after pregnancy. In a RAND Corporation study of the employment decisions of women born between 1957 and 1965, over 70 percent were still employed at the same job six months following childbirth, and another 11 percent were employed with a different employer. When focused solely on women managers and professionals, the study found that 92 percent were still employed six months after childbirth.[4]

In a time of increasing longevity, however, children are not the only family members who need care. Eva Feder Kittay reports that a quarter of all American families are caring for an elderly relative or friend—doing all those concrete, intimate, and time-consuming details of embodied care, from changing adult diapers to shopping for groceries and making visits to the doctor's office. These caregivers are overwhelmingly women.[5] They pay an emotional and economic price. Over 60 percent of those caring for an elderly relative reported bouts with depression. Two-thirds had given up promotions and training opportunities related to their employment.[6]

These statistics describe a sea change in the lives of mothers, children, women caregivers, and dependent persons that has not been sufficiently calculated into the mainstream Christian vision of gender equality.

WHO CARES FOR CHILDREN WHEN MOTHERS GO OFF TO WORK?

The following data are provided by the U.S. Census Bureau in its report "Who's Minding the Kids? Child Care Arrangements, Fall 1995" (hereafter abbreviated USCB) and by the Urban Institute's study "Child Care Patterns of School-Age Children with Employed Mothers" (hereafter abbreviated UI).[7] These reports investigated childcare arrangements during the school year for those hours parents (mothers in a dual-couple marriage) worked or went to school.[8] About a quarter of all preschoolers (below age five) have a parent (mother) who is not employed and who, presumably, takes care of her preschool-age children (USCB). Of all preschoolers, 75 percent use some form of regular arrangement for childcare in a typical week. Of all preschoolers, 44 percent regularly use two or more arrangements during a week.[9] Preschoolers of working parents spend an average of thirty-five hours per week in some form of childcare. If cared for by nonrelatives, as most preschoolers are, preschoolers average thirty-nine hours of care per week. Relatives, especially grandparents, are more likely to provide the secondary arrangement. If cared for by daycare centers or family daycare providers, preschoolers average thirty-three hours of care per week. Preschoolers in low-income families (families whose income is below the poverty line) and preschoolers of never-married mothers are more likely to be cared for by relatives than nonrelatives. Very young children (two years of age or younger) are more likely to be cared for by babysitters or family daycare providers than by organized daycare centers.

In the 1995 school year, school constituted the primary childcare arrangement for virtually all school-age children (between five and fourteen years of age) in a typical week. However, a variety of gaps exists between the schedules of working parents and children's school hours. Parents typically have to be at work before, during, and after school hours. Parents, especially those employed in low-pay work, may work nontraditional hours. School holidays often do not mirror holidays in work schedules. Consequently, according to the USCB, it is typical for school-age children of working parents to be cared for by more than three childcare arrangements in a week. Of these school-age children, 52 percent are regularly cared for by a nonparental relative during nonschool hours. Twenty percent of these children regularly spend some time each week in self-care, and 18 percent regularly spend time in nonrelative care. Thirty-five percent of these children participate in organized activities, called enrichment activities, while their parents work. These activities include before- and after-school programs, sports, clubs, and lessons such as music lessons.

Enrichment activities are the second or third arrangement for 54 percent of the children of working parents. Children in nonpoor families (families whose income is above the official poverty rate) are more likely than children of poor families to spend time in activities that would, as the USCB report states, "assist their development and transition to adulthood." Income level also impacts the type of enrichment program children may use. Before- and after-school programs in poorer urban areas take the place of sports and music lessons in the suburbs.[10]

As children grow older, the use of self-care increases. About 40 percent of twelve- to fourteen-year-olds spend between five and ten hours per week alone; another 16 percent spend more than ten hours in self-care. Family structure, labor force participation, and income impact the amount of time school-age children spend alone. For example, the USCB found no significant difference in the likelihood that children of a single parent will be in self-care than will children of a dual-earner, married couple. (Children of single fathers were found to spend significantly more time in self-care than were children of single mothers.) However, children whose parents are employed are more than twice as likely to use self-care as are children of parents who are not employed. The UI study found that the group with the highest percentage in any amount of self-care is the ten- to twelve-year-olds of fully employed single parents. It is not surprising that parents with less time are more likely to leave children in self-care. More surprising, perhaps, is the finding that children in self-care are more likely to live in families with incomes higher than the average income of families with children (USCB). Self-care is used the least in two-parent families in which one parent is not employed and in single-parent families in which the parent is not employed.

The UI study concluded that while most children appear to be in a supervised setting during mothers' working hours, a significant minority of children care for themselves. The likelihood of self-care increases with age and is more likely among older school-age children of higher-income, white families in which the mother works traditional hours. The study is not able to determine whether these patterns of self-care are due to the preferences of parents or whether they are choices based on the only available options. However, the UI study noted that other research indicates "that children who are left alone are at greater risk of physical injury and psychological and emotional harm." Since the data are based on self-reporting, there is also the possibility that time spent in self-care is being underreported.

Children in Michigan reflect many of these national trends. Michigan children (under five) of employed mothers spend thirty-five or more hours in childcare and typically depend on two or more childcare arrangements. Michigan infants and toddlers (under three), whose mothers are employed, are more likely than the national average to spend time in childcare. Children of low income families are less likely than children of higher income families to spend time in childcare and are more likely to utilize only one arrangement—typically relative care.[11]

These reports highlight the multiple arrangements and their coordination that working mothers depend on each week in order to provide care for their children. Yet, each report only studied childcare arrangements during the typical school year. Left unanswered is what working mothers do during summer months, during school vacations, or when children are too ill to go to their primary care arrangement. Each study also makes explicit in its methodology that childcare becomes an issue because of the employment of mothers. By design the employment of fathers is not part of the data collected except in those rare cases where the father is a single custodial parent. The implicit understanding is that it is *mothers* at work who create the childcare problem.

THE PUBLIC CONTEXT OF PRIVATE CHOICES

These data reveal that despite the dependence of millions of mothers on the childcare arrangements that make their wage work possible, and despite the dependence of U.S. employers on women workers, childcare in the United States remains a private family problem. In the public/private ideology that characterizes contemporary U.S. society, family life is presumed to be a private realm where individual freedom and privacy should be protected from the intrusion of the state.

In reality, of course, positive and punitive laws and government policies have supported the gendered division of labor that defines men's privileges by assuming the normality of only the bourgeois nuclear family. The Social Security Act of 1935 is a good example. Married men, paying the same tax as single men, receive much greater benefits: income insurance for their wives and children as well as old-age benefits for their wives. The program is essentially designed to reduce the cost of family responsibilities for a married breadwinner. Today most wives work. But because they typically earn less than their husbands, they are likely to opt for Social Security benefits based on his earnings. In that case, her Social Security benefits are based neither on her nonmarket work nor on her market work.[12]

The state also intrudes into procreative decisions, typically justified by calling into question the ability of certain women to act responsibly, as determined by those who are more affluent, white, and male. In the 1930s, at a time when white women were denied legal access to contraception and abortion, the public health departments of southern states took the lead in developing contraception projects designed to reduce the pregnancy rates of black women.[13] Today, TANF (Temporary Aid to Needy Families) is explicitly designed to impact the childbearing choices of economically poor women based on (false) assumptions connecting welfare, poverty, and irresponsible childbearing. Placing a "family cap" on welfare assistance reflects the "common sense" that single, economically poor women receiving government assistance irresponsibly choose to have more children. By 1999 more than twenty-three states had done so despite the data showing that since 1975 the average welfare family had two children—the same as the national average.[14] The common sense of the political economy is not easily shaken by the lack of empirical data to support its claims.[15]

Nonetheless, the dominant ideology describes the choice to have children as, in most instances, a private choice. Of course, the personal choice to have children, how many, and when, is expected to be made responsibly; that is, a woman is expected to take into account the impact of childbearing on her life plans. She is expected to understand the impact that childbearing will have on her commitment to wage work. Thus, while Americans in general support gender equality in the workplace, they support women's employment only up to a point. Surveys find that 82.1 percent of Americans believe that "women are biologically better-suited to care for children." Moreover, 67.8 percent believe that everyone benefits when women "take the main responsibility for the care of the home and children, while men take the main responsibility for supporting the family financially."[16] Consequently, employed married women are expected to put unpaid domestic work and childcare work before their commitment to a wage job. In addition, married women's wage work is not to supersede husbands' roles as primary earners of income.[17] Despite attestations of gender equality, responsibility for childcare is a mother's problem. Responsibility for dependent care is a woman's problem.

The point, of course, is that U.S. culture sees the work of care for children and other dependent persons as a matter of private choice—a *woman's* private choice. But far from being an issue of private choice, it is a social arrangement creating injustice. By describing childbearing as solely the individual choice of a woman, this ideology provides a commonsense way of justifying her responsibility for bearing privately whatever social consequences may come of that choice. Understanding parenting as a private choice justifies the rejection of most social responsibility for children by U.S. public policy.[18] It justifies punitive social policies for low-income single mothers.

The coercion and injustice underlying this social pattern have been masked by two ideological assertions. One is that women are naturally predisposed to be caregivers. By naturalizing dependent care as a feminine gender characteristic, this argument hides the coercion that history reveals was necessary to restrict modern women's options. The second assertion is that care of dependents is part of the private realm, of family and personal choices. This argument justifies the lack of any social responsibility for both dependents and their caregivers as a result of their free "personal" choices. In reality, women choose to become mothers despite knowing that this places them in a position of greater social vulnerability than that of men who choose to become fathers. And mothers enter the labor force to work for wages despite knowing that the conditions under which they work will be more burdensome than those of fathers. Women who care for children and dependent others know that they enter the competition for economic and social goods handicapped. This is not an exercise of free choice but the determination to do the best one can despite the lack of fairness that structures these options. That women survive, "manage," even prosper under unjust conditions does not justify the injustice.

Furthermore, two material realities are masked by the fictions of human autonomy and free choice. First is the reality that no society lasts beyond this generation without procreating. The second is that every member of this generation has been dependent on the caregiving of another and will likely be dependent on caregiving again. The denial of these social realities permits the establishment of social institutions based on the normality of individual autonomy and choice. Only one other great fiction has exercised such social power: that man (Zeus, Adam) gave birth to woman. The consequences of these ideological assertions and the social arrangements that they justify weigh heavily on all women whether or not they have children or other dependents. As Carol Robb succinctly states: "Whether or not they are mothers, women are subject to discrimination in the labor force because they *can* be mothers."[19] At work and at home women encounter a gendered division of labor that unjustly increases their economic vulnerability and, consequently, their economic dependence on men. The irony, of course, is that those most responsible for creating gender-equal and family-friendly work environments or for legislating social policies are those least likely to experience the need.[20]

SOCIAL CONSEQUENCES

Unequal Access to the Work Force

One consequence of the gendered division of dependent care is the inequality of women's access to employment and its benefits relative to men's. A vast number of studies have documented the negative impact of the lack of affordable and available childcare on all women's employment, regardless of their occupation and status. Women work less than they would like and have to disrupt their work more than men do because of childcare concerns. These concerns are expressed in two ways. One concern is that having childcare is not all that being a parent is about. Parenting, regardless of income level, has to also include the time and attention necessary for a good relationship.

> *I make about two hundred dollars a week, which isn't bad for twenty-five hours. My aunt and everyone say, "Why don't you find a better job, one with benefits and all that?" Well, when she is little like this I'd rather work twenty-five hours and get that amount of money, than work more and not spend time with her. That, to me, is more important.[21]*

The other concern is related to the cost, availability, and quality of childcare:

> *I need to work during the day so I can be here with my kids at night. Minimum-wage pay and an evening job where I would have to pay a baby-sitter is not worth it. It's more trouble than it's worth and in the long run I would be making out worse. They would take away my medical and my food stamps and my kids would lose me.[22]*

These are not only the concerns of low-income mothers. A recent study of managers in the ten industries that employ the most women raises the issue sharply. First, the study found that 60 percent of women managers did not have children, but for men the figure was reversed: 60 percent of male managers did have children. Second, during the boom times of the 1990s, the salaries of these women managers lost ground in relation to those of male managers in five of the ten industries. More troublesome, mothers lost the most ground. While women tend to be paid equally with men up to about the age of thirty-three, they steadily lose ground after that, with mothers losing the most in comparison to fathers. Once women managers start families they earn only 66 percent of what managers who are fathers are paid.[23]

For some women, simply being able to leave children for employment is a significant problem. One study reports that 10 percent to 20 percent of nonemployed American mothers with young children do not seek employment because of the lack of childcare availability and affordability[24]

> *It's hard to tell the employe[r] when I can start because I can't get child care until I get a job. There's waiting lists at least 15 names long at most places and day care without abuse/neglect complaints that are affordable are few and far between.[25]*

The same study also found that 20 percent to 25 percent of employed mothers would work more hours if childcare were not an issue. In 1994, the Bureau of Labor Statistics documented the hidden involuntary part-time employment of 850,000 people who were classified as *voluntary* part-time workers but who worked part-time because of problems with childcare.[26]

Because of the cost of childcare, low-income, married-couple families often cannot afford to send a second worker (typically the mother) into the wage labor force if that second income does not significantly, and imme-diately, add to the family's well-being. Thus, the cost of childcare weighs against the employment of wives. The two-earner strategy that sustains the income of middle-income families often has to be abandoned by low-income families. Research indicates that in households where husbands are unemployed, lack of cash income may also force wives to withdraw from the labor force. Employment creates direct costs, such as transporta-tion, clothing, and meals, as well as the indirect cost of losing the value of wives at-home work.[27]

> We were finding, for what I was making, I couldn't pay a sitter and pull out any extra money. It just wasn't worth it, and that's why I'm doing what I'm doing today—being home with the kids.[28]

Another study looked at the relationship between the availability of childcare and the stability of mothers' jobs. It found that mothers who had to rely on spouses' care or child self-care were 2.2 times more likely to leave a job than mothers using organized childcare centers. The same study found a positive impact on the stability of women's work when mothers had access to convenient and affordable center-based childcare.[29] Low-income families are obviously disadvantaged in sustaining their paid-work efforts because of their need to rely on care provided by family friends and relatives.

> My family provides child care and I give them what I can. Different ones take care of them different times and days. . . . I don't want "just anybody" watch-ing my kids.[30]

Childcare instability is aggravated by gender and class hierarchy. Women experience more work disruption because of childcare problems than do men. But blue-collar male workers report more childcare related work disruptions than do male executives.[31] Even among dual-career, attorney couples, "the husband's schedule is deemed to be more demand-ing than that of his wife, and she is expected to fill in the gaps in child care."[32] Women, in general, and even couples trying to sustain egalitarian family relationships, are caught in a dilemma created by the assumption that neither government nor the economy has a responsibility to help working parents care for children and other dependent persons. Since such work is still assigned by social arrangements primarily to women, women pay the price of greater economic vulnerability because of unequal access to consistent employment.

My kids are first. My kids are always first. Basically everything I work for or think of working for is around them . . . the hours, the pay, the kind of work I do—all the decisions revolve around them.[33]

Unequal Access to Quality Care for Dependents

A second consequence of viewing the care of dependents as a private issue is its impact on the quality of childcare. A class hierarchy is created when childcare is treated as a commodity in the marketplace, like cars or cloth-ing or toys. As a commodity, market forces determine the cost, quality, and availability of care that most parents would consider of inestimable value. This results in an unequal impact on women and their families of the financial cost of childcare and unequal access to quality care. These inequalities are unjust because they function to sustain class and race dis-parities in family well-being—disparities that undermine even the ethi-cally minimal claim to equal opportunity.

I worked in child day care for approximately a year. Kids are never taken care of the way they should be. . . . Putting 15 kids in one area of the school for 8 to 12 hours a day with the care of qualified person is not the best of a child interest. As a matter of fact, I had just graduated high school. . . . I was left all by myself, while their teacher was wasting her time in the office with the director. That goes to show you how kids are left with peo-ple without experience. These days there are too many problems associated with day care and babysitters.[34]

Nationally, families bear the bulk of the cost of childcare—60 percent. Ninety-six percent of working parents pay for childcare solely out of their own pockets. Government provides another 40 percent of the cost of childcare through subsidies to low-income families. Private industry con-tributes less than 1 percent of the national cost of childcare.[35] What does childcare cost? Albelda and Tilly, in a 1995 survey of childcare centers, found that full-time care for a preschool child ranged from a low of $217 a month ($2,604 annually) in Mobile, Alabama, to $589 a month ($7,068 annually) in New York City. After-school care costs one-third to one-half as much.[36] A more recent survey by the Children's Defense Fund reports that childcare for a four-year-old in a childcare center averages between $4,000 and $6,000 per year. Infant care is typically $1,100 more per year. However, elite childcare centers may charge upwards of $10,000 per year. Family childcare is generally less expensive (and mostly unregulated and unsupervised) but still averages over $4,500 for a four-year-old. And while costs tend to be somewhat lower in rural areas, the cost of center care for a preschool-age child still falls between $3,000 and $6,000 per year.[37] In Michigan, the cost (1997) of childcare for a four-year-old in a center averaged $5,000 a year. This exceeded the annual cost of tuition at a public university in the state. It would consume well over half of the annual income (pretax) from a full-time minimum wage job.[38]

Who can afford to pay? A study of eighty-five lawyers and their families in the New York area provides a concrete example of the hierarchy even within high-earning families. Of the highest earners, thirty-six attorneys making more than $150,000 annually, twenty-five used full-time, live-in nannies. Some of these also employed housekeepers and other domestic staff. Lesser earning lawyers, $100,000 to $150,000 annual income, turned to part-time nannies and organized daycare centers. And those with the least income ($75,000 to $100,000) turned to daycare centers and baby-sitters. All of the lawyers depended upon, expected, and paid for extremely flexible and committed childcare providers.[39]

> *I have . . . a tremendously flexible arrangement, both the after-school for him and a sitter [for her toddler] for as long as I need her. She's tremendously flexible. If she has some appointment, she'll clear it with me. And then I'll know that I absolutely have to be home by then. Otherwise it's easy to sort of bleed into 7 o'clock without trying hard.*[40]

However, since the median family income in 1999 was $48,950, most families, even with two working parents, do not have the financial resources to copy any of these high-income solutions.[41] What is a serious and expensive need for middle- and upper-income families is a crisis for low-income families. Lack of financial resources, by definition, keeps low-income families at the bottom of the childcare market. The result is that some children are being left in inadequate care as mothers try to sustain wage work. According to a statement released by the White House in

December 2000, "states were able to provide childcare assistance to only 12 percent of all federally eligible low-income working families" in 1999.[42] Essentially, nine out of ten low-income children who are eligible for childcare subsidies do not get help. The U.S. Census Bureau estimates that low-income families who paid for childcare spend 35 percent of their incomes on childcare, compared to 7 percent of income spent by nonpoor families.[43] These figures become more meaningful when compared to women's income. A woman who earned the average hourly wage for single women nationwide in 1997 ($9.71) received $20,200 gross annual pay. If she lives in Boston, or New York, or Minneapolis, or Philadelphia, she would have to spend one-fourth to one-third of her gross salary on organized daycare.[44]

> I was going to let my five-month old son . . . go into day care . . . but this being such a big city they have a bad reputation here for child care. And child care looks like a dump yard on the outside so I can just imagine what it looks like on the inside—and then DFCS, the family and whatever, only pays so much so that means that you have to go to the lower class places. You know, the places that looks more bummy or everyone in there is so alley and so I'd rather not work in the daytime. . . .[45]

The impact of the childcare market on low-income families is further illustrated by the Michigan Assemblies Project (MAP) survey of 1,700 low-income families and 500 community institutions. Michigan welfare-reform law requires that mothers work once their infants are thirteen weeks old. The average cost of full-time childcare in Michigan is $4,500, or 44 percent of the gross earnings from a full-time, minimum wage job. Of the employed respondents, 60 percent earned less than $7 an hour ($14,000 annually for full-time, full-year employment). Only one-fourth of the families surveyed received any state subsidy for childcare, and only one-half of those reported that the subsidy covered childcare cost. Most used a friend or relative for childcare; most were dissatisfied with their childcare arrangements; and half had lost time at work because of childcare problems. Children thirteen years old and older are not covered by state subsidies, and almost half are at home alone while parents work; another third are with friends.[46] Yet, Michigan has seen its daycare subsidy caseload grow from approximately 25,000 cases in 1995 to about 72,000 in 1999. The cost of its program has tripled in the same years.[47]

With the growth of service work, the number of people working odd-hour shifts is also growing. Since lower-wage mothers are more likely than other workers to work nonstandard hours, they also face greatly increased problems of childcare availability, dependability, and affordability.[48] In Michigan, less than 1 percent of licensed daycare providers are open on weekends. Only 1 percent will care for children overnight; about 2 percent accept sick children. Michigan's poor parents, like those in other states, are often in an odd-hour squeeze because they must accept the work they can get, typically low-paying and low-skill jobs.[49]

> When I work nights it's hard. . . . They get lonely and a bit worn down. . . . They get tired of being grown up, basically, is what they are when I am gone. Every night you go to bed and think of the hundreds of things you could have done better.[50]

Consequently, the financial well-being of single mothers is directly linked to their ability to balance wage work and family-care responsibilities—a balancing act now attempted by more and more economically poor women with less and less social support. Economically poor mothers negotiate that balance on a daily basis. Rarely does the public discourse about poverty and single-parent families take seriously this connection between dependent-care work and wage work. A study of one Midwestern urban housing project makes the connections dramatically.[51] Health problems of family members make extraordinary demands on the time of these poor single mothers. Of the fifty-six resident mothers, 30 percent reported that someone in their household suffered from a serious disease, such as lupus or cerebral palsy; 28 percent reported other less serious health problems. Almost 40 percent of the mothers reported being involved in the care of a member of their family not living in their own household, giving evidence of the impact of strong kinship ties and greater longevity on dependent-care responsibilities.

In this urban housing project, the reality of urban gang violence also shaped each day's childcare activities. These mothers protected their children through constant, strict supervision and by avoiding public activities. Protecting their children meant being present each day to walk with them to and from school and all other activities.[52] This commitment to their children meant that the time available for wage work was limited to a few hours in mid-day or to night hours if proper childcare could be found. The type of flexible employment that fits in with the child- and dependent-care responsibilities of these mothers is typically low-wage and no-benefit employment—when it can be found.

> Most job[s] I obtain, I have to make sure that the hours are suitable to work around my son's school schedule. Most of those types of jobs are too far out for

me to travel to. By me remaining local, I'm limited to very low paying jobs with no room for advancement. . . . My child goes to school from 9:30–3:50. He has to be at the bus stop at 8:45 and he gets home at 4:30. At those times, I am at work. I work from 7:30–4:30. My family members also work similar hours. So, I had no one to take my child to the bus stop or pick him up.[53]

However, neoliberal public policies directed at economically poor families take shape around the sole goal of employment. There is widespread social agreement that economically poor mothers cannot, by definition, be good mothers *unless* they work away from their homes and their children. Lawrence Mead thinks poor mothers are poor because of passivity, and Governor Kirk Fordice told reporters in Mississippi that all welfare recipients needed was a "good alarm clock."[54] Economically poor single mothers are vilified if they do *not* do wage work. And despite the differences in access to material resources prescribed by parenting experts, they are vilified if their children do not achieve according to middle- and upper-income standards. Yet, at the same time that Congress imposed work requirements on single-mother families with preschool-age children, with *infants*, it repealed provisions that had guaranteed childcare to low-income families. No state is required to provide assistance to pay for childcare.[55]

On the same day that the White House admitted the gross inadequacy of state subsidies for childcare, the Children's Defense Fund released a study of 5,000 families who had left welfare since 1996 but sought help in 1999 from local community agencies that provide homeless shelter, emergency food, and other services targeting the poorest. Looking specifically at those families who had children under the age of eighteen, the CDF found that 44 percent were headed by a working parent, 58 percent of whom had weekly earnings below the poverty line. Less than 30 percent of these families were receiving help paying for childcare. Of those parents who had left welfare for work and were no longer working, the most frequently cited reason was lack of childcare (36 percent of all unemployed parents in the study).[56] The CDF's findings are repeated in any number of smaller studies aimed at determining what low-income families are experiencing.[57] Without providing an adequate income or adequate government subsidies for childcare, social policies that demand "work first" leave the children of low-income workers at the bottom of society's hierarchy of care. Congressional back-slapping celebrating reduced welfare rolls and increased poverty-level employment makes political points. It makes no moral sense.

In the short term, of course, these social policies are economically rational. Low-income mothers are the cheapest source of childcare for their own children as well as for the children of others. Public policy assures that their participation in the labor force will be unstable as they miss work to care for their own children. The economy gains a source of low-income, disposable workers and saves the cost of providing adequate childcare and material necessities for family well-being.[58] But in the long run, such policies make no economic sense if the impact on people and communities of overwhelmed lives is taken into account. For example, medical researchers are increasingly looking at the negative outcomes of persistent stress—lifetime stress. Connections are being made between lives stressed by fear of violence, money worries, and job insecurities and the persistence of racial disparities in infant mortality, problem pregnancies, and low-weight births. While direct causalities are most difficult to prove, suspicious correlations exist between the stressed context of lives lived in deprived socioeconomic communities and the poorer outcomes for children raised in such circumstances.[59] The maintenance of such harsh conditions can only be explained ideologically. As a living morality play, the deprivation of poor (especially black) women provides a stern warning to any woman who contemplates divorce and motherhood outside of patriarchal marriage. It sustains America's racism while disciplining all women.

Viewed differently, economically poor single mothers are like the canary in the mine. They reveal the basic incompatibility between wage work and caregiving in a political economy where the labor of care for one's own dependents is not valued as work and where the cost, quality, and availability of childcare and dependent care are left to market forces.

> OK, I had gotten a part-time job from 5 P.M. to 9 P.M. . . . . It was like a four-hour position. My daughter started failing in her grades. 5-9, $6 an hour—really. . . . So what I did was that I left that position, for her. Because I felt like she was accustomed to having me there, so, you know, to help her with her homework. . . . So I left that position and the state terminates me, completely. . . . So she went up in her grades, thank the Lord. But we lost our monies and so forth.[60]

Unjust Connections among Women and Families

Feminist scholars typically use the term "reproductive labor" to refer to all those activities involved in carrying out the functions assigned to families. It includes the activities of nurturance, as well as the activities of providing, processing, and maintaining food, clothing, shelter on a daily basis, and all the activities of socialization. Central to feminists' analyses of women's oppression has been the recognition that the social assignment of these functions to women has been a crucial component of men's exploitation of women's labor.

At the beginning of the twenty-first century, several factors have converged to commodify an ever-increasing number of these reproductive activities. One factor is simply the nature of capitalism to constantly seek new areas of production from which to make profit. Another is that over time new products and services reshape how things are done so that they simply become necessary for modern life—ovens, refrigerators, microwaves. People lose the skills to do what their grandparents once did for themselves—raising, killing, and plucking chickens for dinner, for example. For some of this commodification, we can all be grateful. However, the particular focus here is the influx of women, especially white, middle-and upper-income women, and especially mothers, into the formal labor market. As Macdonald and Sirianni state:

> . . . the feminization of the work force has created a self-fulfilling cycle in which the entrance of more women into the work force has led to increased demand for those consumer services once provided gratis by housewives (cleaning, cooking, child care, etc.), which in turn has produced more service jobs that are predominantly filled by women.[61]

Commodified or not, reproductive labor remains women's work.

As a commodity, childcare has become a growth industry in the expanding service sector of the U.S. economy. The "toddler/industrial" complex is dominated by large chains such as KinderCare Learning Centers, Primrose Schools, and La Petite Academy. It has also spawned an industry of suppliers like Childcraft, Beckley, Apple, and Kompany.[62] Between 1977 and 1992 the number of childcare facilities nationwide doubled and the number of paid employees in the childcare industry more than doubled (190,000 to 468,000). Between 1992 and 2001 the number of licensed childcare centers increased from 86,212 to 111,506. Recession in the beginning of the twenty-first century has merely slowed the rate of growth.[63]

High-quality childcare is consistently related to several factors: the educational level and training of employees, small group size, low attendant-to-child ratios, and wages. Yet, from 1977 to 1992, the wages of childcare workers decreased in constant 1992 dollars from an average of $10,161 in 1977 to an average of $9,251 in 1992 (less than $6 an hour).[64] The *Detroit*

News, in a special report on daycare, quoted a 1999 survey of daycare centers in Detroit, Atlanta, Boston, Phoenix, and Seattle showing that workers earned between $6 and $10.85 per hour. The median wage of childcare-center workers in 1997 was $7.03 per hour, three cents less than that of parking lot attendants. Paradoxically, the average childcare worker cannot herself afford the average cost of childcare. Low wages also contribute to the fact that, in Michigan, for example, nearly 30 percent of the children in daycare lose their caregiver every month—a rate consistent with the nationwide turnover rate of one-third of childcare employees annually.[65] In essence the childcare industry has pursued a low-wage, low-benefit, and minimal-training policy.[66]

Given this expansion of low-wage work, the direction taken in welfare reform in 1996 appears not only wrong-headed, but perverse. Under TANF any job is considered a step out of welfare, including "the provision of child care services to an individual who is participating in a community service program." In other words, one welfare recipient providing childcare to another welfare recipient's child is working, but caring for one's own child is not.[67] In the stampede to reduce welfare rolls, without regard to whether poverty and its deprivations are reduced, low-income mothers are urged to become the poorly paid caregivers of the children and dependents of others. They are also, of course, those who provide the services and products which middle- and upper-income parents must now purchase in order to sustain the needs of their families: fast food, domestic cleaning services, Sunday retail shopping, commercial janitorial services, mail-order and e-mail-order distribution and mailing services, and so on.

As in the past, a racial/class division continues to characterize reproductive work that is performed for wages. Evelyn Nakano Glenn has carefully documented the racial stratification that exists within women's wage work:

> Racial-ethnic women are employed to do the heavy, dirty, "back-room" chores of cooking and serving food in restaurants and cafeterias, cleaning rooms in hotels and office buildings, and caring for the elderly and ill in hospitals and nursing homes, including cleaning rooms, making beds, changing bed pans, and preparing food. In these same settings white women are disproportionately employed as lower-level professionals (e.g., nurses and social workers), technicians, and administrative support workers to carry out the more skilled and supervisory tasks. [68]

These are the invisible workers crucial to making middle- and upper-income standards of living possible. Not seeing these women supports the illusion that meals appear, bathrooms become clean, silicon chips are made, blackboards are washed, waste cans are emptied, and people are cared for without human effort. The cruel innocence of the privileged remains intact.

> *It pays $5.70 an hour. . . . Basically the job is to give care to the residents of the nursing home. We wash them, we feed them, we take them to the bathroom. You have to lift them out of bed, into their wheelchairs. . . . I'm most proud of the fact that I'm actually doing something for all these people who can't do something for themselves. Last night there were two ladies in the hallway. One was in the wheelchair and wanted to go to bed. Another lady passed her and said, "Ask Susan to put you to bed. I know she will, she's a nice girl." She didn't realize I was standing there. That's the proudest thing to me, to know that they know they can count on me if they need help. . . . I'm still afraid of the death and dying part.*[69]

As in the nineteenth century today's privileged families continue to purchase the goods and services needed to sustain a material standard of living that protects "family values." Today it can be done with minimal personal contact. Good families can display the virtues of good parenting by purchasing quality childcare, an infinite range of enrichment activities, family vacations, private education, or well-supported public education. Good parents buy prepared foods, expand wardrobes, select the best educational toys, and readily turn to the services of child therapists and marriage counselors. The commodification of reproductive services permits this while erasing from view the economic relationships that connect the lives of good families to the lives of the women—a disproportionate share of whom are women of color—who are unable to make this standard of care possible for their own families. The issue briefly caught the public's attention in the "nannygate" scandal associated first with one of President Clinton's nominees, Zoe Baird, and, later, with a George W. Bush nominee, Linda Chavez. Media attention focused on the employment of undocumented women of color by women who were being considered for major positions in law and labor policy. The question raised was about the character of these individual women. But these cases illustrate the layers of social inequality. Educated and successful woman resolve work/family conflicts by exploiting other women. Men simply are not held responsible for childcare arrangements and family labor. And now unjust relationships between women become global because of economic disparity among nations. All over the world, poor women from the periphery leave their own families to care for the children of women (and men) in the overdeveloped world. Globally, the arrangement makes economic sense.

The servants live like church mice in cities like Los Angeles and Rome, and
wire their earnings home. This supplies their countries with billions of dollars of foreign currency, opens a valve against the mass frustrations of
poverty, and pays draconian debt service on loans from the World Bank or
International Monetary Fund. Meanwhile, the servants' own kids are hun-
dreds or thousands of miles away in the poor countries, where someone else
is raising them at far less cost than if they had followed their mothers
abroad.[70]

As more and more family activities are commodified to save time for
better-employed women, by what theory of justice do middle- and upper-
income women secure their own well-being and that of their families while
poor women provide cheap labor at the cost of *their* families' well-being?[71]
In addition to the moral prohibitions that arise from the norms of distributive justice, Fred Glennon has argued convincingly that these work relationships also violate the standards of commutative justice: shared
meanings, mutual competence, and the prohibition against harm.[72] In
addition, they sustain the ideological basis of gender inequality, the
devaluing of reproductive work, by using racism or classism to blind
middle- and upper-class women, most of whom are white, to their own
continuing, gendered vulnerability. Audre Lorde named the temptation of
privileged women. It is "the pitfall of being seduced into joining the
oppressor under the pretense of sharing power."[73]

Uh, I worked at McDonald's for a year and a half. . . . And we would stay up
there two-three o'clock in the morning cleaning, and it was like it was for min-
imum wage. They would give us what they called a raise, which was only like
anywhere from five to ten cents, like, you know, please. . . . My beginning pay
was $4.25. My ending pay was $5.35.[74]

THE NEW NANNY CORPORATION

In response to the crisis in the quality and availability of childcare, the
1990s saw a growing interest in the various ways that business could adopt
childcare as part of the responsibility of employers to their employees.
With very low unemployment rates, tightening economic pressures
encouraged employers to document the cost of childcare problems in
terms of lost time at work and employee turnover rates. Research institutions were founded and popular magazines offered articles identifying the

most family-friendly corporations on the basis of their response to parental needs. According to Peter Berger, corporate capitalism has now created a new ideal—a kinder, gentler capitalism, a caring institution. This new, caring corporation is evidenced, he says, by on-site daycare, elder care, health and counseling programs, and so forth. The modern corporation has become "a sort of private-sector incarnation of the welfare state—the 'nanny corporation.' . . ."[75] Others may not be quite so rhapsodic; but many mainline Christian ethicists share the belief that modern corporations can become institutions that embody covenantal virtues.[76] If that is true, it seems reasonable to inquire into the practices by which these nanny corporations have facilitated the equal participation in employment of women and men with caregiving responsibilities.

Direct Services

The primary response of larger firms has been to provide employees with referral services to already existing community resources. Few businesses have decided to provide childcare facilities directly. In its 1997 National Study of the Changing Workforce, the Families and Work Institute found that 12 percent of employees with children under six reported having access to a childcare center provided or sponsored by their employers at or near their workplace. [77] Only 9 percent of over one thousand businesses surveyed with more than one hundred employees reported providing childcare on or near the work site.[78]

However, in November 2000 the most aggressive corporate response to childcare concerns was announced by the Ford Motor Company, Visteon Corporation and ZF Batavia (Ford's part-supply partners), and the United Auto Workers. The plan called for the development of a network of corporate "Family Service and Learning Centers" in thirty communities and fifteen states.[79] These centers, many now open, provide a wide range of family-oriented programs for the employees and retirees of these companies, who are UAW members, and their children. Local family councils, composed of UAW members, determine the specific menu of programs for each center. For example, a center might include grief counseling, personal-growth seminars, community-service activities, teen programs, a library, banking assistance, and tutoring. Thirteen of these centers include childcare facilities, each with a capacity of 220 children, paid for on a fee-for-service basis by the employee. Each of the childcare centers operates twenty-four hours a day and seven days a week, if needed. They provide full-time, part-time, back-up, and school-age care, as well as care for children who are mildly ill. Back-up and mildly-ill care is available for children six weeks to twelve years of age.

This extensive and innovative program, however, is not the result of corporate nanny-ism. It is the result of direct labor negotiations between the UAW, Ford Motor Company, and its suppliers. The UAW/Ford Joint Program fund provides 71 percent of the funding. The other 29 percent is company money. Consequently, in the recession that hit Ford in 2002, resulting in plant closures and the layoff of thousands of workers, the family centers could not be touched. They were safe as part of a signed union contract. The UAW considers this program an example of what strong unions can accomplish for their members and it would like to see this approach replicated through other unions' activism.[80]

Without union pressure, other much more modest corporate initiatives were also underway in 2000. For example, in October, Abbott Laboratories initiated a small back-up care program that will cover nine holidays over the school year. It is also constructing an on-site center that will offer childcare at market rates for 425 children from infants through preschoolers.[81] It remains to be seen whether initiatives, unprotected by union negotiations and contracts, will survive economic recession.

Organizations such as the Families and Work Institute see the provision of corporate childcare as a positive response by the business community to the work-family stress of parent-employees. Parents would no longer need to be concerned about school holidays or a failed childcare arrangement or even a sick infant. Work hours could be met knowing that one's children were being cared for nearby.

Christian ethicists may wish to pause and reflect on the implications of all this. They should remember the benefits and problems created by the development of company towns in the last century. Company towns often employed teachers and preachers for their employees and their families. They provided retail stores and housing. But the very provision of these supports to civil life were also means of worker control in the face of increased union and socialist activity. Today, highly acclaimed corporate campuses mark the new high-tech knowledge companies that employ the more highly educated worker. Work, accessorized by exercise rooms, concierge services, fully stocked kitchens, nap tents, and childcare—at least for some workers—seems kinder and gentler. But when the well-being of one's children becomes ever more closely tied to a particular employer, especially where legal and unionized protections of workers have become weak, Christian ethicists should question the controls exercised by velvet reins.

Decisions to change jobs or to challenge working conditions, including hours and wages, will be harder for parents to make. In fact, from the perspective of business, the oft-stated reason for providing childcare is to gain more employee loyalty, time, and productivity. Since employment in the new economy has become more unstable, as employers replace traditional employment security with the new employability contract, childcare tied to one's place of employment will also become less stable. What kind of childcare is available when one's job has been downsized and plants moved to other countries? Recent history has shown that the corporate trend is to reduce employment benefits so that a greater proportion of both cost and risk is placed on workers. So, to the extent that responding to childcare concerns was a response to an unusually tight labor market, it is likely that a loosening of the labor market or a down turn in the economy will dull corporate interest. Corporate-sponsored childcare remains a line item in an activity focused on producing capital. It remains, like working parents, subject to the logic of a capitalist market.

There remains an additional concern. Many public intellectuals and Christian ethicists argue that the moral quality of nations requires strengthening civil society: that arena of institutions in which nonmarket values are learned in the intimacy of family, neighborhood, and voluntary associations. It is that environment where particular traditions and their values are passed down to the next generation. Nonmarket values are expected to be the core of an individual character formed within the institutions of civil society. Shaped by nonmarket values, persons of character are expected to provide moral limits to the drive of self-interest valued in the marketplace. How is this distinction to be maintained if employers become the providers of family services—of infant and after school care, and teen activities? Whose values will shape our children?

What appears to be a caring corporate response may be the erosion of any pretense of distinction between civil society and the economy. Where there used to be a professed valuing of family life for infants and children, and family-shaped holiday observances, and time at home with a caring parent for the mildly ill, now there will be corporate life for infants and children, with corporate-designed holiday observances, a corporate crib for the fussy six-week-old, and a corporate cot for the six-year-old who is mildly ill. This solution, as well as the growing profit-oriented business of childcare, serves the needs of business much more than it serves the well-being of families and the work of moral formation. The scenario of more family adults in the work force, more family hours spent doing wage work, and more children in the care of corporate and for-profit childcare centers is especially troubling to those whose family values are not reflected in the common sense of a capitalist society.

Financial Support

Other corporate responses to childcare concerns have included programs that enable employees' use of helpful provisions in the tax code. In the Families and Work Institute's 1998 Business Work-Life Study, 50 percent of companies reported providing dependent-care assistance plans that help employees pay for childcare with pretax dollars. However, such accounts are generally available only in public-sector employment and in large businesses with over one hundred employees. Consequently, according to the Bureau of Labor Statistics, only 30 percent of workers have access to them.[82] Just 5 percent of businesses reported providing vouchers or other types of subsidies that are a direct cost to the business. Only 12 percent of employees surveyed in the 1997 National Study of the Changing Workforce reported receiving childcare subsidies in the form of vouchers, cash, or scholarships from their employers to help offset part of the cost of childcare.

In an attempt to increase the supply and quality of childcare, the U.S. Department of Health and Human Services created the Child Care Partnership Project. The state of Florida provides an example of one type of public–private partnership funded by this project: the "Child Care Executive Partnership." Faced with twenty-five thousand families on a waiting list for state-subsidized childcare, the state of Florida entered into a partnership with businesses in which the state matches employer contributions for childcare to employees whose *household* income is less than 150 percent of the federal poverty level. The poverty threshold for a family of three in 1998 was $13,133 and $16,530 for a family of two adults and two children. In 1998 thirty-five businesses participated in the partnership, which is billed as a "win–win" situation. "More low-income families can maintain stable employment without the worry of affording childcare; employers benefit from less employee absenteeism and turnover; and the state of Florida is able to provide more eligible families with childcare subsidies."[83]

Of course, the common sense behind such partnerships requires submission to the logic of capitalism. When wage levels are considered to be just because they are the product of the impersonal forces of supply and demand in a competitive labor market, the cost of workers' childcare needs escapes the calculation. After all, low-skilled workers could (should?) choose to refrain from having children. Or they could increase their skills and command more wages from the marketplace. According to this logic, contributions from the state, derived primarily from taxing higher-income workers, are considered a handout to the working poor. More-affluent taxpayers typically resent seeing their "hard-earned" income being redistributed to the poor. Governments find themselves under pressure from business interests as well as individual citizens to reduce taxes. The result is a no-win situation in which such programs will constantly be subject to budgetary restraints. It takes no seer to predict that the childcare needs of low-wage workers are not likely to be adequately funded in this way. Nonetheless, the company may describe itself, or be described, as "family friendly" because of the voluntary expense it incurs on behalf of its low-paid employees. The state is likely to believe that it is doing all it can afford to do for low-income families. Only from an alternative perspective is it possible to point out that the cost of labor has been socialized.

One such alternative perspective is the attention that has been given in the Roman Catholic tradition to workers' right to a living wage. Christine Firer Hinze quotes Msgr. John A. Ryan's explanation of the return that is due the laborer: "Food, clothing, shelter, insurance, and mental and spiritual culture—all in a reasonable degree—are, therefore, the essential conditions of a decent livelihood."[84] Ryan did not contemplate the possibility that women, particularly mothers, as well as men would also be laborers. But Hinze argues that to apply Ryan's understanding of a living wage to today's context requires "a 'family living wage' (an amount sufficient to reasonably support self, spouse, and children) for every adult wage worker, male or female, regardless of marital or family status."[85]

The demand that workers be paid a wage adequate to support the worker and his or her family has been made by Christian denominations throughout the twentieth century. Nonetheless, the share of workers earning poverty-level wages has increased since the 1970s from 23.6 percent in 1973 to 26.8 percent in 1999.[86] When business does not pay a living wage to some workers, and when the rest of society has to share its income to make up the deficit, the cost of labor has been *socialized*—not to the benefit of the common good but to the benefit of profit-making corporations. Yet the ideology of capitalism remains intact, unquestioned, including its deprecation of the poor, who are disproportionately women and children.

I worked at the coat sewing factory for almost two years. Everything had to be perfect, not a stitch out of place. . . . You weren't allowed to talk to the people who sat beside you. . . . It was a forty-hour-a-week job and then I worked half-time on Saturday. It was a good-paying job. I made pretty good money. It started out minimum wage, but it was piece rate. If you sat there all day long, except for your half-hour break, you'd make seven or eight dollars an hour. . . . They just sit there all day long. They don't even get up and go to the bath-room.[87]

The Child-Friendly Workplace

There is one final innovative response to childcare that merits mention. In the tight labor market of the late 1990s some businesses began to permit employees to bring their infants to work. The Kansas Insurance Department, a law firm in Chicago, a personnel agency in Ft. Lauderdale, a bank in California, and eighty-five companies out of five thousand surveyed in Ohio permitted workers to care for their babies while they work. Media pictured high chairs behind bank tellers and cribs beside data-entry clerks to celebrate this new corporate receptivity to the concerns of new mothers. Employees are quoted as happy to work at a company where they can bring their infants to their workstations. Employees can hold, feed, burp, bump, cuddle, and bounce their babies while talking to irate customers by phone, answering e-mail, taking customer orders, and opening accounts. Such employers are considered "enlightened." When the unemployment rate was 4 percent, the market logic behind this move was simple. As one CEO said, "I know they will be distracted. Still, being here even at 60 percent is better than totally missing that person."[88] It is also better than having to retrain another person. "Better," of course, is defined by the economic rationality of a capitalist market. It means "less expensive" for the employer. It means being a 40 percent mother is better than the alternatives: losing one's job or enduring the stress of inadequate or costly or unreliable childcare. The problem is that economic logic defines what is good for children now that women, in the name of equality, are redefined as wage workers.

This is the new reality of childcare, of child rearing, in the postindustrial, neoliberal, U.S. economy. Despite the counsel of best-selling parenting guides that children need "intensive mothering," the political economy makes work necessary for most mothers and demands it of poor single mothers. For those who can afford it, work–family conflict is resolved by *relieving* mothers and fathers of their *own* children's care. For thirty to forty hours each week, someone else sings the songs, reads the stories, and teaches the traditions to most preschool children. Someone else readies children to take their place as adults in a democratic society.[89]

Yet, as the cost of child and dependent care increases, a neoliberal political economy rejects that cost through stagnating wages, the reduction of government assistance to low-income families, and resistance to publicly funded policies that would better balance the demands of employment with home life. It is families, especially women, who are left to bear these costs alone. Racialized gender stereotypes ease an ideological transition in which work that serves the accumulation of capital becomes central to the lives and identities of all. Gender stereotypes continue to mask the basic problem: an economy hostile to the "feminine," to that which attends to human well-being in relationships of mutual interdependency.

NOTES

1. Thomas E. Lengyel, ed., *Faces of Change: Personal Experiences of Welfare Reform in America* (Milwaukee, Wisc.: Alliance for Children and Families, 2001), 174. The speaker is a twenty-nine-year-old printer living in Buffalo, New York. *Faces of Change* is a research project in which the stories of persons touched by welfare reform were recorded.

2. Karen Schulman, "The High Cost of Child Care Puts Quality Care out of Reach for Many Families," *Issue Brief* (Washington, D.C.: Children's Defense Fund, 2000); www.childrensdefense.org/childcare/highcost.pdf. Ann Crittenden, *The Price of Motherhood: Why the Most Important Job in the World Is Still the Least Valued* (New York: Metropolitan Books, 2001), 277 n. 8.

3. Sheila B. Kamerman, "Parental Leave Policies: An Essential Ingredient in Early Childhood Education and Care Policies," *Social Policy Report* 14, n. 2 (2000): 3. In 1970 only 27 percent of mothers of infants were in the labor force.

4. Jennifer Glass, "Do Mothers Stay on the Job?" *Research-in-Brief* (Washington, D.C.: Institute for Women's Policy Research, March, 1996).

5. Eva Feder Kittay, *Love's Labor: Essays on Women, Equality, and Dependency* (New York: Routledge, 1999), x, 204 n. 142. Kittay reports that in a 1985 survey about 33 percent of part-time workers spent more than twenty hours a week helping older relatives, while 27 percent of previously employed people had taken early retirement, or resigned, in order to care for relatives. A 1997 survey reported that twenty-two million elderly persons were being cared for by a relative, almost always a woman, who spent an average of eighteen hours a week in unpaid care work. Of these caregivers, 25 percent spent forty or more hours each week giving care (Crittenden, *The Price of Motherhood*, 275 n. 6). While the focus of this chap-

ter's discussion of caregiving will be on children, the growing need for adults to care for aging parents should remain in our vision.

6. Nancy Folbre, *The Invisible Heart: Economics and Family Values* (New York: New Press, 2001), 37.

7. Kristin Smith, "Who's Minding the Kids? Child Care Arrangements, Fall 1995," Current Population Reports (U.S. Department of Commerce, U.S. Census Bureau: October 2000); available at www.census.gov/population/www/socdemo/childcare.html; and Jeffrey Capizzano, Kathryn Tout, and Gina Adams, "Child Care Patterns of School-Age Children with Employed Mothers," Occasional Paper No. 41 (Washington, D.C.: Urban Institute, 2000) available at http://newfederalism.urban.org/html/op41/occa41.html.

8. Less than 5 percent of preschool-age children and less than 3 percent of school-age children were affected by mothers' schooling.

9. "Arrangements" refers to the use of relatives, organized childcare facilities, or nonrelatives. A lack of "regular" arrangements during working hours may indicate instability in childcare arrangements or difficulty in determining what arrangement is most regular. Nonrelatives refers to in-home babysitters, family daycare providers, and other nonrelatives providing care in the provider's home (USCB).

10. See, for example, Jodi Wilgoren, "The Bell Rings but the Students Stay, and Stay," *New York Times*, 24 January 2000: A1, A18.

11. "Child Care in Michigan: 1997 Snapshot," Kids Count in Michigan, a project of the Michigan League for Human Services and Michigan's Children, Lansing, Mich.

12. Folbre, *Invisible Heart*, 96–99. Other governmental actions include legislation that defines "family" and all of the laws and policies that presume such a definition: tax laws, inheritance laws, pension and unemployment coverage, immigration policies, jail visitation privileges, and so forth. See Nancy F. Cott, *Public Vows: A History of Marriage and the Nation* (Cambridge: Harvard University Press, 2000).

13. John D'Emilio and Estelle B. Freedman, *Intimate Matters: A History of Sexuality in America* (New York: Harper & Row, 1988), 247–48.

14. Mimi Abramovitz, *Under Attack, Fighting Back: Women and Welfare in the United States* (New York: Monthly Review Press, 2000), 37–39. Other examples would include the forced childbearing of black female slaves in the nineteenth century—protected by the state under the prerogatives of private property; the ongoing, long history of women's struggle to legalize the knowledge and practice of contraception (most recently RU486); the continuing struggle to safeguard and extend access to safe, medical abortions; and the current TANF legislation providing federal funding for abstinence-only sex education.

15. Empirical studies show no correlation between welfare benefits and pregnancies. European countries generally provide much greater support for single mothers than does the United States, yet have much lower birthrates. Higher-benefit states within the United States do not have a correspondingly higher rate of unwed births. Further, the real value of government assistance has consistently

fallen since 1973. Kristin Luker notes the few studies that have shown a weak correspondence that varies by ethnic group and specific contexts (Luker, *Dubious Conceptions: The Politics of Teenage Pregnancy* [Cambridge: Harvard University Press, 1996], 126–27). See also Michael B. Katz, *The Undeserving Poor: From the War on Poverty to the War on Welfare* (New York: Pantheon Books, 1989), 153, 215–23; and Stephanie Coontz, *The Way We Never Were: American Families and the Nostalgia Trap* (New York: Basic Books, 1992), 258–61.

16. Sharlene Hesse-Biber and Gregg Lee Carter, *Working Women in America: Split Dreams* (New York: Oxford University Press, 2000), 197–200. Data taken from the *General Social Survey, 1994–1996* (Chicago: National Opinion Research Center, 1997).

17. Emily Kane and Laura Sanchez, "Family Status and Criticism of Gender Inequality at Home and at Work," *Social Forces* 72, no. 4 (1994): 1079–1102; and Jane Riblett Wilkie, "Changes in U.S. Men's Attitudes towards the Family Provider Role, 1972–1989," *Gender and Society* 7 (June 1993): 261–79. In a survey of one thousand employees 66 percent of the respondents said that one parent should stay at home to raise the children; 94 percent of the women expected that their partner would work for pay; 66 percent of the men expected their partner to work for pay. See "Life's Work: Generational Attitudes Toward Work and Life Integration," available at www.radcliffe.edu/pubpol. See also Crittenden, *The Price of Motherhood*, 26.

18. U.S. public policies that support the cost of childraising are income tax exemptions and the child tax credit which help families with a taxable income; TANF and the Earned Income Tax Credit aid low- and no-income families.

19. Carol Robb, *Equal Value: An Ethical Approach to Economics and Sex* (Boston: Beacon Press, 1995), 27.

20. Most senior executives are white males insulated from the demands of caregiving by secretaries, personal assistants, and wives. Public policies are determined by legislative bodies overwhelmingly white, male, and affluent. Crittenden, *The Price of Motherhood*, 231.

21. Virginia E. Schein, *Working from the Margins: Voices of Mothers in Poverty* (Ithaca, N.Y.: Cornell University Press, 1995), 76.

22. Ibid., 46.

23. Elizabeth Becker, "Study Finds a Growing Gap Between Managerial Salaries for Men and Women," *New York Times*, 24 January 2002: A22.

24. Harriet B. Presser and Amy G. Cox, "The Work Schedules of Low-educated American Women and Welfare Reform," *Monthly Labor Review* 120, no. 4 (1997): 25–28.

25. Lengyel, ed., *Faces of Change*, 215.

26. Barbara Hilkert Andolsen, *The New Job Contract: Economic Justice in an Age of Insecurity* (Cleveland: Pilgrim Press, 1998), 44.

27. Margaret K. Nelson and Joan Smith, *Working Hard and Making Do: Surviving in Small Town America* (Berkeley: University of California Press, 1999), 70, 46.

28. Ibid., 71.

29. Sandra Hofferth and Nancy Collins, "Child Rearing and Employment Turnover: Child Care Availability Increases Mothers' Job Stability," *Research-in-Brief* (Washington, D.C.: Institute for Women's Policy Research, March, 1997).

30. Lengyel, ed., *Faces of Change*, 118.

31. Cabral, Brummit, and Levin, "Child Care Problems and Worker Productivity: An Examination of Gender, Occupational Status and Work Environment Effects" (Detroit: Merrill-Palmer Institute, 1996).

32. Cynthia Fuchs Epstein et al., *The Part-Time Paradox: Time Norms, Professional Life, Family and Gender* (New York: Routledge, 1999), 109–10.

33. Schein, *Working from the Margins*, 46.

34. Lengyel, ed., *Faces of Change*, 109.

35. Anne Mitchell, Louise Stoney, and Harriet Dichter, *Financing Child Care in the United States* (The Ewing Marion Kauffman Foundation and the Pew Charitable Trusts, 1997); summary available at www.pewtrusts.com/pubs/misc/childcare.cfm.

36. Randy Albelda and Chris Tilly, *Glass Ceilings and Bottomless Pits: Women's Work, Women's Poverty* (Boston: South End Press, 1997), 56–59.

37. Karen Schulman, "Issue Brief: The High Cost of Child Care Puts Quality Care Out of Reach for Many Families," Children's Defense Fund 2000, December 2000; available at www.childrensdefense.org/childcare/highcost.pdf.

38. "Child Care in Michigan: 1997 Snapshot," Kids Count in Michigan, a project of the Michigan League for Human Services and Michigan's Children.

39. Epstein et al., *Part-Time Paradox*, 109–10.

40. Ibid., 111.

41. Median family income for married couples in which the wife participated in wage labor (47.6 percent of all families) was $66,529 in 1999. For those married couples in which the wife was not in the wage labor force (29.2 percent of all families), the median family income was $38,626. Lawrence Mishel, Jared Bernstein, John Schmitt, *The State of Working America 2000–2001* (Ithaca, N.Y.: Cornell University Press, 2001), 47.

42. Child Care Statement, Office of the Press Secretary, December 6, 2000; received from www.beta.pcusa.org/pipermail/wo-hunger-hu/2000-December/000041.html

43. Smith, "Who's Minding the Kids?" According to the Census Bureau, in 1995 those with annual incomes below $18,000 paid about $71 weekly for childcare; those with annual incomes of $54,000 and above paid about $101 weekly.

44. Albelda and Tilly, *Glass Ceilings*, 59. The median incomes of full-time, full-year women workers range from $10,200 to $24,133 depending on race/ethnicity. Teresa Amott and Julie Matthaei, *Race, Gender and Work: A Multi-Cultural Economic History of Women in the United States* (rev. ed.; Boston: South End Press, 1996), 348.

45. Lengyel, ed., *Faces of Change,* 104. DFCS refers to the speaker's state Department of Family and Children's Services.

46. Michigan Assemblies Project, *Welfare Reform: How Families Are Faring in Michigan's Local Communities* (Detroit: Groundwork for a Just World, 1998) 21–27.

47. Michigan League for Human Services, "The Growing Need for Child Day Care and Resulting Budgetary Impacts," Lansing, 1999.

48. Presser and Cox, "The Work Schedules of Low-educated American Women and Welfare Reform," 25–28.

49. B. G. Gregg, "Odd hours, sickness give parents headaches," *The Detroit News,* 7 November 1999. www.detroitnews.com/specialreports/1999/daycare/sunsalaries/sunsalaries.htm.

50. Sally Reid works full-time and as much over-time as possible to support herself and her three children. Terri Heath et al., "Oregon Families Who Left Temporary Assistance to Needy Families (TANF) or Food Stamps: In-Depth Interview Themes and Family Profiles" (Center for the Study of Women in Society, University of Oregon: January 2001), vol. 2, p. 20; available at http://server.fhp.uoregon.edu/csws/welfare/welfvol1.shtml.

51. Deborah L. Puntenney, "The Work of Mothers: Strategies for Survival in an Inner-City Neighborhood," *Journal of Poverty* 3, no. 4 (1999): 63–92. See also Stephanie Moller, "Work, Welfare and the Breadwinning Mother: Incorporating Gender into Structural Vulnerability Theory," *Journal of Poverty* 3, no. 4 (1999): 19–35.

52. One October day, Datrell Davis walked to school with his mother. A sniper in a tenth-floor window of a Cabrini-Green Housing Project, aiming at rival gang members, pulled the trigger and took Datrell's seven-year-old life. June Gary Hopps, Elaine Pinderhughes, and Richard Shankar, *The Power to Care: Clinical Practice Effectiveness with Overwhelmed Clients* (New York: Free Press, 1995), 34.

53. Lengyel, ed., *Faces of Change,* 88.

54. Both cited in Abramovitz, *Under Attack, Fighting Back,* 30.

55. Jo Ann C. Gong, Alice Bussiere et al., "Child Care in the Postwelfare Reform Era: Analysis and Strategies for Advocates," available at www.welfarelaw.org/chcc.htm. Only twelve states exempt poor mothers from the work requirement until their infant is one year old. Mary Jo Bane characterized some of these provisions as "gratuitously punitive" and driven not by social science but by "electoral calculations"—including the decision of President Clinton to sign the bill into law. Mary Jo Bane, "Social Science, Christian Ethics and Democratic Politics," *The Annual of the Society of Christian Ethics* 21 (2001): 35.

56. Children's Defense Fund, "Families Struggling to Make It in the Workforce: A Post Welfare Report—Executive Summary," December, 2000; available at www.childrensdefense.org/CMPreport.pdf.

57. Citizens Committee for Children, "Opportunities for Change: Lessons Learned from Families Who Leave Welfare," January, 2000; available from Citizens

Committee for Children, 105 E. 22 Street, New York, NY 10010. Philadelphia Citizens for Children and Youth and United Way of Southeastern Pennsylvania, "Watching Out for Children in Changing Times," full text available at www.pccy.org/publications. A list-serv for information on welfare reform research is available at WELFARE-L@hermes.gwu.edu.

58. In overhauling welfare, the food stamp program was also cut by $26 billion over a six-year period. Private emergency feeding programs have seen a large increase in participants: more than 23 million in the course of a year compared to 21.4 million in 1997. Twenty percent of New Yorkers visited food pantries in the year 2001. According to a survey conducted by Mathematica Policy Research for America's Second Harvest, the new portrait of hunger in the United States includes working families (40 percent of those receiving aid), families with children (almost 50 percent of the households receiving aid), and women (two-thirds of adult recipients). One-third of recipients received food stamps that covered only about one-half of their monthly needs. Elizabeth Becker, "Shift from Food Stamps to Private Aid Widens," *New York Times*, 14 November 2001: A12. A survey of the homeless in the Twin Cities found that 41 percent of homeless women and men were employed with an average monthly income of $622. Josh W. Fountain, "On an Icy Night, Little Room at the Shelter," *New York Times*, 5 January 2002: A1, A9.

59. Richard Rothstein, "Linking Infant Mortality to Schooling and Stress," *New York Times*, 6 February 2002: A20. Poverty increases the likelihood of poor health and disability, and vice versa. Variables in the health of children (such as the number of hospitalizations, acute illnesses, trips to the emergency room, and the presence of chronic illnesses per child per year) are among the strongest predictors of the length of time women remain on welfare. Sue J. Steiner, "AFDC Recipients and Family Caregiving Responsibilities," *Journal of Poverty* 1, no. 1 (1997): 63–79.

60. Lengyel, ed., *Faces of Change*, 33.

61. Cameron Lynne Macdonald and Carmen Sirianni, eds., *Working in the Service Society* (Philadelphia: Temple University Press, 1996), 2.

62. Crittenden, *The Price of Motherhood*, 204.

63. Barbara Whitaker, "Child Care: An Industry for All Economic Seasons," *New York Times*, 16 December 2001: BU6.

64. Casper and O'Connell, "State Estimates of Organized Child Care Facilities," Population Division Working Paper #21, March 1998. Results based on a 1993 survey by the Census Bureau.

65. B. G. Gregg, "Child Care Workers Paid Lowest Wages," *Detroit News*, 7 November 1999. www.detroitnews.com/specialreports/1999/daycare/sunsalaries/sunsalaries.htm; Schulman, "The High Cost of Child Care."

66. Sana Siwolop, "Threshing the Wheat from the Chaff in Child Care," *New York Times*, 20 May 2001: BU 10. Profit margins in the childcare industry are typically about 4 percent and staffing accounts for 60 percent to 70 percent of a center's costs. See Whitaker, "Child Care," BU6.

67. Mark Greenberg, "Welfare Restructuring and Working-Poor Family Policy: The New Context," in *Hard Labor: Women and Work in the Post-Welfare Era*, ed. Joel Handler and Lucie White (Armonk, N.Y.: M. E. Sharpe, 1999), 33; Gwendolyn Mink, *Welfare's End* (Ithaca, N.Y.: Cornell University Press, 1998), 108–9. States are to permit a good-cause exception to work requirements for single parents with a child under six if the parent can prove to the state's satisfaction that she cannot get suitable informal care or affordable formal care within a reasonable distance.

68. Evelyn Nakano Glenn, "From Servitude to Service Work: Historical Continuities in the Racial Division of Paid Reproductive Labor," in *Working in the Service Society*, ed. Macdonald and Sirianni, 115–56.

69. Schein, *Working from the Margins*, 79–80.

70. Debbie Nathan, "A Long Way from Home," *The Women's Review of Books* 19, no. 4 (January 2002): 3.

71. In classical economics, economic mobility is the answer to this question. Workers who work hard, gain experience, learn skills, and show good work habits will move from entry-level jobs to jobs requiring more skills and paying higher income. However, studies of economic mobility in the United States show (1) that there is no greater economic mobility in the United States than in European countries; and, (2) most people in the United States stay in the income fifth where they began (Mishel, Bernstein, and Schmitt, *The State of Working America 2000–2001*, 386, 75–78). Against the argument that the working poor are poor because they differ in substantial ways from other workers (very young, very old, less educated, or in unusual family arrangements), studies show that many of the working poor are in married-couple families, at their prime working age, have a high school education or more, and work many hours. See Marlene Kim and Thanos Mergoupis, "The Working Poor and Welfare Recipiency: Participation, Evidence, and Policy Directions," *Journal of Economic Issues* 31, no. 3 (September 1997): 707–28.

72. Fred Glennon, "Desperate Exchanges: Secondary Work, Justice, and Public Policy," *The Annual: Society of Christian Ethics* (1992): 225–44.

73. Audre Lorde, *Sister Outsider: Essays and Speeches by Audre Lorde* (Trumansburg, N.Y.: Crossing Press, 1984), 118.

74. Lengyel, ed., *Faces of Change*, 206.

75. Peter L. Berger, "Vice and Virtue in Economic Life," in *Christian Social Ethics in a Global Era*, ed. Max Stackhouse, Peter Berger, Dennis McCann, and M. Douglas Meeks (Nashville: Abingdon, 1995), 87–88.

76. For a concise summary, see Eric Mount, Jr., *Covenant, Community, and the Common Good: An Interpretation of Christian Ethics* (Cleveland: Pilgrim Press, 1999), 81–87.

77. Rima Shore, "Ahead of the Curve: Why America's Leading Employers Are Addressing the Needs of New and Expectant Parents," Families and Work Institute; executive summary available under publications at www.familiesand work.org.

78. Ellen Galinsky and James T. Bond, "1998 Business Work-Life Study: A

Sourcebook," www.familiesandwork.org. The 1997 National Study of the Changing Workforce surveyed a representative sample of employees in the U.S. labor force.

79. "Ford, Visteon, UAW Launch Nation's Most Comprehensive W/F Program," *The National Report on Work & Family* 13, no. 23 (November 28, 2000), 211–12. See also Steven Greenhouse, "Child Care, the Perk of Tomorrow?" *New York Times*, 13 May 2001: WK 20.

80. See www.familycenteronline.org; and union spokesperson, Judy Harden, 313-392-7236.

81. "Holiday Care Part of Comprehensive Child Care Program at Abbott Labs," *The National Report on Work & Family* 13, no. 22 (November 14, 2000), 203.

82. Bureau of Labor Statistics, "Child-Care Benefit to Employee Emerging," 1997; available at www.bls.gov/ebs/cwc3.txt.

83. Quoted from "The Child Care Executive Partnership" found at http://nccic.org/ccpartnerships/profiles/ccep.htm.

84. John A. Ryan, *A Living Wage: Its Ethical and Economic Aspects* (London: Macmillan, 1906), 136, cited in Christine Firer Hinze, "Bridge Discourse on Wage Justice: Roman Catholic and Feminist Perspectives on the Family Living Wage," in *Feminist Ethics and the Catholic Moral Tradition*, ed. Charles Curran, Margaret Farley, Richard McCormack, S.J. (New York: Paulist Press, 1996), 515–16.

85. Hinze, "Bridge Discourse on Wage Justice," 530.

86. The poverty-level wage is that hourly wage that a full-time and year-round worker must make in order to sustain a family of four at the federal poverty threshold (a level most agree is much too low). In 1999 that was $8.19 (Mishel et al., *The State of Working America 2000–2001*, 129–31).

87. Schein, *Working from the Margins*, 73.

88. Pam Belluck, "A Little Bit of Burping Is O.K. If It Keeps Parents on the Job," *New York Times*, 4 December 2000: A22.

89. For a related discussion, see Todd David Whitmore, "Children and the Problem of Formation in American Families," *The Annual of the Society of Christian Ethics* (1995): 263–74.

4

Spending Time
When Time Is Money

We are getting less than 40 hours of work from a large number of our K.C.-based EMPLOYEES. The parking lot is sparsely used at 8 A.M.; likewise at 5 P.M. As managers—you either do not know what your EMPLOYEES are doing; or you do not CARE. . . . In either case, you have a problem and you will fix it or I will replace you. . . . NEVER in my career have I allowed a team which worked for me to think they had a 40-hour job. I have allowed YOU to create a culture which is permitting this. NO LONGER. [1]

THUS READ AN E-MAIL memo sent by a CEO to his managers. The memo went on to list six potential punishments, including the lay-off of 5 percent of the work force if managers did not succeed in getting the parking lot full at 7:30 A.M. and at 6:30 P.M. and half full on Saturdays. The memo boomeranged. After it was leaked and posted on Yahoo, the internet exploded with derisive comments. The business community chastised the CEO for using e-mail as a managerial memo. He was criticized for the tone of the e-mail. Many derogatory comments were directed at the idea of measuring productivity by counting cars in the parking lot. The price of the company's stock dropped 22 percent in three days. However, in this blitz of opinions, one topic was absent—the issue of time. No one argued with the amount of time devoted to work that this CEO expected.

Controlling time, and changing people's sense of time, was central to the development of capitalism. "Lose no time: Be always employ'd in something useful: cut off all unnecessary Action," wrote Benjamin

Franklin.[2] Consequently, one part of capitalism's story has been the success with which employers expanded the discipline of industrial hours over their work force.

The other part has been workers' resistance to that discipline—a resistance that finally resulted after World War II in what most Americans today consider a normal workweek: the eight-hour day and the five-day week. At that time observers of the American scene celebrated the leisure time enjoyed by many Americans, accompanied as it was by rising wages and rising productivity. One expert testified to a Senate subcommittee that by the 1990s, Americans would be enjoying "either a twenty-two hour week, a six-month work year, or a standard retirement age of thirty-eight."[3] So much for experts!

In the new economy, as the value of time increases, so does the conflict over time. There is just not enough time in any one day to go around. The traditional boundaries of time have disappeared. The basic rhythms of the day—waking and sleeping—have lost their meaning. Business hours are twenty-four/seven. Every moment is awake and every moment *works*. Engineering projects subcontracted to workers in India are transmitted before dawn into the still dark and quiet offices of U.S. companies. At any moment, somewhere in the world, a stock exchange is adding and subtracting wealth from portfolios that are always open. Money whisks electronically across continents. Risk and opportunity spar in each moment. There is no rest. There is no time for rest. Time is money. In hindsight, Franklin's horse-powered life of constant industry appears leisurely.

How much time *should* workers work at market-oriented activities? What tempo *should* guide the weave of productive work and family work into a full fabric of meaningful life? Does the assessment of this e-mail change if one imagines a woman as the CEO, women as the managers, or women as the employees from whom greater market-oriented work time is being demanded? How do gender assumptions fit into the tempo of globalized work? How should they?

TIME'S DISCIPLINE IN THE NEW ECONOMY

Twenty-four/Seven

Work Force Flexibility
In the new economy flexibility is the new core value. Every moment must be met with rapid, just-in-time, response. Businesses must be able to trans-

form themselves almost instantly to meet new demands as productively as possible. Companies are frequently hiring even as they are firing in a continuous process of tailoring labor to fit the available work. Flexibility means "that work tasks and work time can be constantly adapted to changing products, processes, and markets."[4]

Indeed, the necessity for a flexible and work-absorbed labor force has become a mantra in U.S. economic discourse. It is used to explain U.S. economic success or the lack of it. During the early months of 2001, the U.S. economy was facing a downturn of uncertain proportion. In comparison, growth in European markets was linked by U.S. pundits to the gradual relinquishing of traditional forms of worker protection. The European choice was presented as maintaining, even expanding, workers' rights as a defense against a firm's new strategies for flexibility or its acceptance of the demands of the new economy. On the front page, the *New York Times* described the European turn to flexibility: "Wage increases have slowed to a crawl and labor markets have become more flexible, as companies skirt traditional job-protection rules by hiring part-time and temporary workers."[5]

For example, in recent years German companies have turned to increased automation, moving factories offshore, and out-sourcing of work, as well as to the use of temporary and "leased" workers, to decrease company size and to avoid the legally protected practice of "co-determination." The choice facing the German government was whether to expand workers' rights to include these downsized, more flexible, companies. Chancellor Helmut Schroeder did in fact sign controversial legislation that extended worker protections to smaller companies. But that legislation did not protect the growing numbers of temporary or "leased" workers. In summer 2001, Siemens, the German electronics company, was able to eliminate over two thousand jobs without paying severance or going through negotiations because the workers were temporary employees with limited contracts. From 1990 to 1998, according to the European Commission, nine out of ten jobs created in Europe were either temporary or part-time jobs.[6]

In the United States, as we have seen, one aspect of the demand for flexibility has been the demise of the traditional labor contract and its replacement by the new "employability" contract. Both the Clinton and the George W. Bush administrations encouraged the concept of free agency for employees, in which companies recognize a responsibility to improve the skills of workers rather than responsibility to provide job security.[7] Now that more employees are required to sign documents acknowledging that they are "employed at will," laying off employees is no longer regarded as a mark of disloyalty or greed. It is simply the new face of business.

In the surge of layoffs that characterized dot.coms at the end of the year 2000 and into 2001, skilled employees typically received no advance notice and often no severance pay.[8] Severance pay, when offered, was often linked to employees' willingness to sign agreements relinquishing their rights to sue their employer—suits, for example, that might be based on employees' suspicions that they were singled out for layoffs because of age or race. Amazon.com offered twelve weeks of severance pay to those who signed releases and only two weeks to those who did not. In 2001, Lucent Technologies paid no severance to laid-off employees unless they signed such a release.[9] Newly laid-off workers, especially those with families, faced a difficult choice between desperately needed income and the uncertain outcome of a legal claim, no matter how valid. In the new economy the flexibility needs of business reestablish the economy's control over workers and their families by abandoning responsibility for them.

Mandatory Overtime
While flexibility results in job loss for some, it results in too many hours at work for others. Nursing strikes in Flint, Michigan, and at Nyack Hospital in New York during the winter of 2000–2001 highlighted the problem of mandatory overtime.[10] Responding both to nursing shortages and to pressure for greater economic efficiencies, hospital administrators used mandatory overtime to handle fluctuations in patient census while maintaining a lean work force. The result was nurses with increased numbers of more critically ill patients under their care being asked to work well beyond the ten hours that most studies show to be the limit for effective nursing care. In Flint and at Nyack, nurses struck against mandatory overtime that required nurses to work two eight-hour shifts, back to back. In response to similar pressures, the Massachusetts Board of Registration in Nursing issued an advisory stating that the refusal to work overtime would not be considered "patient abandonment," for which a nurse can lose her license. Of course, the life and death context of the nursing practice usually results in public support when the issue is overtime. Workers in other occupations of service or production may not get as much sympathy from a harried public.

At the height of its success in the late 1990s, Amazon.com enforced mandatory overtime work of at least ten hours a week for its second-level customer-service representatives. These tier II workers were expected to work a minimum of fifty hours a week. The work pace was to be "at Amazon time," or on "uptime," terms meaning an intense work pace with min-imal interruptions and maximum efficiency. Time pressures were part of the reason for some workers' attempt to unionize these college-educated, hourly-wage earners in the new economy.[11]

The millennial year saw eighty-five thousand telephone workers strike Verizon Communications. The issues included job security, benefits, unionizing of the lower-wage employees of the new economy, and time. One employee, Patricia Egan, wanted measures that would help reduce stress and the use of forced overtime.

> We generally work from 8 in the morning until 4, but often we're forced to work until 8 at night. It wreaks havoc. People go to school and they're forced to miss classes. Many workers are single parents, and this forced overtime is a night-mare. It creates serious problems for their child care arrangements.[12]

Mindy Fried describes this singular focus on work as a "culture of over-time." Fried studied ten large corporations, all of which were participants in a national organization focused on family and work issues. One large financial services corporation has at its corporate headquarters over seven thousand employees, two-thirds of whom are women. It has a large menu of family-oriented policies. Fried was studying, as she put it, the best-case scenario.[13] Yet, Fried found that while the company provided information about its policies, it did not promote them. In subtle ways the clearer mes-sage was that in a business crisis, the best employees were those who set all else aside for the sake of the company. A daily corollary to that message was the commonsense managerial view that the more time an employee gave to the job, the more productive she was. Employees who took family leave or who resisted overtime, men or women, were rated down in merit-pay evaluations because such evaluations were based on time-oriented mea-sures of productivity. Recent experiences with layoffs had made employees fearful. In a business climate of mergers, out-sourcing, and downsizing, each feared giving any impression that might make one seem to be the more "disposable" employee.

While this company's official thirty-seven-and-one-half-hour work-week looked good on paper, in actuality, its employees worked over forty hours a week. On paper, this company's generous parental leave policy included eight weeks of *paid* maternity leave. Yet, few managers, and no male managers, had used it between 1992 and 1995. Men did not even con-sider taking leave at the birth of a child. Even among nonprofessional employees, the culture of overtime was so internalized that those who took some leave returned as quickly as possible to their jobs in order to prove their commitment and loyalty, and to make up the time they had lost. Long hours at work, "face time," was viewed as necessary behavior to save one's job. Fried concludes that it is the workplace culture, not the work/family policies, that determine the use of leave time for family needs. She quotes a human resources manager:

> *We work all the time. Whether you're working or not, you're here all the time. We're trying to shift this, but people feel, "I'm going to lose my job if I'm not here." People are afraid to go to a reduced schedule. "If I'm not here, what will happen?"*[14]

Working Longer for Less

In 1991 Juliet Schor, an economist, caused a stir by announcing that the average American worker had added 164 more hours (a month's worth of work) to the work year between 1970 and 1990. She further estimated that a quarter of all full-time workers was working forty-nine or more hours per week.[15] American workers had surpassed the workers of all other industrialized nations, even Japan, in the amount of hours per year spent in employed work.

Almost a decade later, Schor's basic thesis of an overworked American labor force, which had not gone unchallenged, received new support.[16] The Economic Policy Institute estimated that in the decade from 1990 to 2000, each family had added three more hours of work a week to their yearly total—an addition of 156 hours.[17] The International Labor Organization, a United Nations agency, confirmed that the 1,979 hours that U.S. workers worked in 2000, on average, is almost nine full weeks more than most European workers. It is about twelve and one-half weeks more a year than German workers, and three and one-half weeks more than Japanese workers.[18] Part of this increase in market-oriented work came at the expense of vacation time, holidays, and other forms of paid leave. In the decade of the 1980s, while European workers were securing their four-week, or more, paid vacations, U.S. workers actually lost paid time off per year.

The rest of the increase came from simply putting in more hours at the job. Louis Uchitelle, citing a 1999 Labor Department survey, states that at least 19 percent of the private-sector work force is working forty-nine hours per week or more.[19] Those who work on fixed salaries, he writes, are being stretched "off-the-clock" into many more hours at the workplace for no extra pay. Additional "off the clock" hours include the uncounted time that workers spend on their laptops, cell phones, home computers, and fax machines. Employees "work" in cars, planes, and trains, not to mention homes.

Schor and others argue that families pay the cost when members spend more hours at the job with less time for personal and domestic needs—like sleeping, eating, family provisioning, and attention to children, the ill, and the aged. A 1999 report from the Council of Economic Advisors states that since 1969 U.S. parents have twenty-two hours less each week to spend at home, on average, primarily because of the shift in mothers' time from work at home to employed work.[20] A study of how parents distributed household and market labor hours between 1971 and 1991 supports this contention. On the one hand, the study clearly shows the advantage to families' time when one job generates enough income to sustain a middle-income family life. As "traditional" male-earner families aged and children grew up, the total number of hours spent in all work declined. Husbands tended to decrease the number of hours spent in market labor while increasing substantially the number of hours spent in household labor; wives generally decreased the number of hours they spent in household labor as children became adults.

On the other hand, dual-earner families, particularly those in which wives contributed more than 25 percent of the family's income over the twenty-year period, added approximately six hundred hours of market labor and reduced their household labor by about five hundred hours. According to the authors of this study, the significant decrease experienced in the real earnings of men in these families had to be offset by a significant increase in wives' earnings. Fewer hours were spent in household labor overall because, while men increased their share, it was still far less than that once contributed by women. For most families, then, the cause of increased working hours is economic. As the real wages of men have remained relatively stagnant, "having a single wage earner becomes an increasingly untenable option for most families."[21]

Delaying Retirement

Even at the end of a long life of work, company time seems to be expanding. From the 1950s until the late 1980s, American workers retired at ever-younger ages in large part because of employment-related pensions and medical coverage offered by firms that were encouraging older, more expensive employees to retire. Today, a larger percentage of people over sixty-five are still employed than at any time since 1979 (12.8 percent in 2000). Why the change? Certainly the desire of healthy people to continue working is part of the reason. In addition, the tight labor market of the late

1990s made older workers attractive once more to employers. But, economists also point to the growing numbers of workers who simply cannot
afford to retire.[22] A *New York Times* poll of 1,124 adults in February 2001,
in the heat of a deep market downturn, found a large majority of respondents worried about whether they were setting aside enough money for
retirement. The percentage of respondents who were planning to work
beyond age sixty-five increased to 20 percent (from 14 percent in 1995)
with most identifying finances as the reason.[23]

In the new economy's tightening of efficiencies, retirement benefits also
have been cut. In 1980, 84 percent of full-time employees working for
medium and large companies were covered by defined-benefit pension
plans. In 1995 that figure had dropped to 52 percent. What has increased
is the use of tax-deferred savings plans, like the 401(k). While these are
portable, they are financed mostly by employee contributions out of current wages and carry with them the risks of the stock market. The collapse
of the Enron Corporation in 2001 revealed the risk of 401(k)s that become
too heavily invested in one company—a practice often encouraged, even
required, by some companies' formulas for contributions. While vesting
requirements (the number of years of employment necessary before
employees own corporate contributions) vary, forfeiture rates are high,
especially where job longevity is short. For example, in 1999 the forfeiture
rate at the "Limited," a retail clothing store, was 35 percent.[24]

Moreover, the employee-financed system provides a good deal less for
retirement. When added to Social Security, the traditional employer-
financed plans provided a retirement income at age sixty-five of about 60
percent of the typical worker's pre-retirement pay. 401(k)s added to Social
Security provide a typical pension that is less than 50 percent of pre-retirement pay to people who can expect to live longer than ever before. One
economist estimates that to collect 60 percent of pre-retirement pay, and
to collect it through age eighty-four, today's retiree needs to work four and
one-half more years—to age sixty-nine and one-half. Thus, the new retirement age is somewhere between sixty-eight and seventy years of age.[25]
While it is too soon to tell whether this is the beginning of a long-range
trend, the total length of one's work life may be increasing for middle- and
lower-wage workers.

Producing New Workers

Michael Novak described the change in time consciousness that capitalism
required, the shift from sleepy agrarian time to capitalism's always-awake

time, as part of a new spirit—the spirit of democratic capitalism. He wrote approvingly:

> Under the goal of a better future time came to exert a discipline over the natural rhythms of the body and the psyche. The pace of human life seemed to quicken. Economic activities were no longer oriented merely toward survival or sufficiency but toward a kind of spiritual goal. They acquired purposiveness. The new sense of time demanded abnegations of the body and the emotions not unlike the mortifications of the monks at their monastic "hours."[26]

As capitalism once replaced the sun with the clock and disciplined workers with its bell, so in the transition to the postindustrial, flexible, global form of capitalism, time is again being restructured. Time-as-money, in an ever-faster cycle, again reshapes the lives and virtues of workers. In this new environment, flexible workers are those who are agile in time and place. They absorb the cost of efficiency by being capable of rapid response, longer hours, shorter job tenure, interfirm and intrafirm mobility, wired networking, and constant updating of skills. Pauline Borsook describes the successful entrepreneur who thrives in this economy as a personality

> which needs little downtime, which must be narrowly focused and not prone to self-doubt, which will do all and anything to succeed, which tirelessly and compulsively must act like the greatest salesman in the world, which by definition is workaholic, which risks (and maybe devalues) family life and health. . . .[27]

For most workers, the pressure to stay long hours comes from more intense competition, the new form of job instability under the employability contract, and the new packaging of work into "projects" with tight delivery times. One IBM manager described life in the 1990s:

> You couldn't get to your e-mails during the day, so you'd do them at night. It was like you didn't have a home life. IBM gave you a computer at home. That made it easy to work. I used to pride myself on thinking, I'm not going to complain. I can take it all on. I can do anything.[28]

As most of us can testify, a deeply ingrained psychological element accompanies our increasing hours at work. As the pace of employed work speeds up so does the rest of life's activities. A routine expectation develops that all those involved in meeting our needs should speed up as well. Many admit a growing impatience with slow service, slow computers, slow fax machines, slow traffic lights, and airport delays as expectations about time speed up. According to one labor economist, "We have incorporated the longer hour into our self-image and we have come to accept that to be really successful you have to work a lot of hours."[29]

At the same time, flexible workers must also be able to receive unfazed the pink slips that are now part of the normal work experience.[30] A recent edition of the *Harvard Business Review* displays the new respectability given to the decision to lay off workers as a standard business practice— not the last resort of previous times. At issue is simply the question of how to get workers to work harder. The older answer, represented by one article, stressed employee loyalty.[31] But the new business culture accepts layoffs as a first response. In this culture workers work hard not out of loyalty but out of their own self-interest that, with the constant threat of layoffs, is finely tuned. According to one economist, "Companies are finding that they can achieve their goals by maintaining a certain level of fear in the work force that leads people to work hard."[32]

According to management consultants Laurence J. Stybel and Maryanne Peabody, the promise to employees is freedom. Workers have been freed from the limitations imposed by company loyalty. Workers are now free to think primarily about their own success, to make those choices that enhance their own personal goals and develop their individualized portfolio of skills. Restraints of loyalty, of ties to a company, are replaced by commitment to one's self and one's success in achieving greater and greater employability. They write: "Do not allow yourself to develop the view that you are indispensable to your company or that company is family."[33] In his book *Only the Paranoid Survive*, Andrew Grove, CEO of Intel in the 1990s, agrees: "The sad news is, nobody owes you a career. Your career is literally your business. You own it as a sole proprietor. . . . It is your responsibility to protect this personal business of yours from harm. . . ."[34] Similarly Martin Carnoy argues that the requirements of the new economy shape a "new breed of young professional" who "is constantly on the lookout for a better job, and is ready to jump firms if he thinks there is any chance his present employer might downsize him out of work." Workers, according to Carnoy, become "increasingly autonomous in the work process."[35] This employment instability, that is, "freedom," also changes the nature of work relationships:

> The job and everything organized around the job—the group of friends in the company, the after-work hangouts, the trade union, and even the car

pool—lost their social function. They are as "permanently temporary" as the work itself.[36]

In changing the nature of employment, the new economy creates the demand for a new moral character. Agility, taking risks, and a willingness to disconnect quickly triumph over loyalty and stability. Temporary relationships that add a new experience or a new skill are more valuable than long-lasting relationships. The new economy, as Carnoy bluntly states, is "a way of work and a way of life. Its core values are flexibility, innovation, and risk.... it infuses old industrial cultures with these values."[37] Management gurus and the new outplacement industry join the chorus with a pleasing lyric celebrating the new free agency of employees: "What you offer is You Inc...."[38]

Job insecurity and layoffs are what economists consider natural and inevitable. In the new economy, they are what corporations call "career-change opportunities," or "schedule adjustments," or "force management," or "releases of resources." For employees, however, what is sold as "freedom" is still unemployment, underemployment, and the loss of family stability that good work provides. It is what many workers describe as an assault, a living death, a label of shame.

> I used to work in engineering [as a] technician, I worked there for the last four years and last summer they were having a shakedown, what they were doing was getting ready to have another layoff, so they didn't want to lose me apparently, so they brought me back down into production into the tool room. They froze my pay and dropped me back two pay grades, two levels, and red circled my pay. It was like having to go back to fifth grade. And I'm not kidding you. I mean . . . it's just like somebody said, "You aren't capable of teaching so you've got to go and learn all over again." And this is just the way it feels to me.[39]

Nor have the effects on income of an involuntary job loss changed in the last two decades. In good times and bad, workers who are laid off average an 11 percent cut in earnings compared to what they would have been earning had they stayed in their original jobs.[40] Moreover, the promise of increased employability is hollow. Of those who lost their jobs between 1995 and 1997, about 40 percent of those who gained reemployment earned less than they had at their previous jobs. After reemployment 25 percent took more than a 20 percent cut in income. More experienced workers saw the greatest decline.[41]

Not everyone shares the managerial enthusiasm for the life and character of the new worker. One critical worker typed out this description of work in the high tech industry:

the computer industry eats people, consumes them whole . . . their Dockers-
and-button-down clad minions push and push and push the people who do
the actual work until stomachs writhe in the acid and sleep disappears and
skin goes bad and teeth ache. . . . People who work eight hours a day then go
home to families and lives are derided as not being "team players."[42]

As we have seen, this is not a condition confined to the high tech workplace. It is in the financial services corporation, the health care system, the
white-collar sweatshop, the varieties of service occupations, and everywhere that more is expected to be done by fewer people who cannot afford
to give and cannot expect to receive workplace loyalty. Most of those who
have lamented the increase in "expressive individualism" among American
women and men have pointed to the failings of civil society as the source
of a growing emphasis on the self. But if people become what they must
practice daily, if people pursue the characteristics that receive social
acclaim, then the practices of the new economy provide a stronger explanation for the growth of "Me, Inc."

Whose Choices?
While her announcement of increased time spent in employed work
received the most public attention, Schor was actually asking a deeper
question: "Why has leisure been such a conspicuous casualty of prosperity?" This increase in working hours was not required, she argued. It was a
choice. Schor claimed that increased worker productivity would allow the
United States to produce a 1948 standard of living in less than half the time
it took to be produced in 1948. We could choose to live in comfortable
modern surroundings, particularly compared to most of the rest of the
world, and still have a good deal of free time. A choice had been made. Of
course, no one had asked most Americans to weigh the benefits and costs
of the decision to produce more and more consumer products—and to try
to consume them.

Perhaps it could be argued that American workers do prefer to work
more hours in exchange for always-newer consumer goods. But multiple
surveys do not sustain that argument. One survey of over one thousand
employees between the ages of twenty-one and sixty-five, commissioned
by the Radcliffe Public Policy Center, describes how increases in employed
time impact people's real lives:

* One-third of these employees reported working forty hours a week;
  another 45 percent work more than forty hours a week.

* In families with a full-time worker whose spouse is also employed, 77 percent of the spouses are working forty hours per week or more.
* Only 27 percent of these workers get the recommended eight hours of sleep a night, or more. Forty percent said they needed more sleep.
* Forty-two percent agreed, or strongly agreed, that work–life balance is a problem.
* When asked to name what would help balance work and family needs, 70 percent cited flexible hours; 69 percent cited a four-day workweek; 56 percent wanted fewer hours in the workweek; and 50 percent named having an office at home or telecommuting.[43]

Despite the concerns of workers, it is very clear that reducing the accelerated pace of production in goods and services is not an option in the new economy. In 1989 Schor wrote a letter to three hundred business leaders advocating a shorter workweek. None saw this as a possibility. She quotes a typical response.

I cannot imagine a shorter work week. I can imagine a longer one both in school and at work if America is to be competitive in the first half of the next century.[44]

In a 1993 *Fortune* magazine survey, 77 percent of the CEOs polled believed that global success will require pushing managers even harder.[45] The experience of workers confirms that the philosophy of working harder while earning less shapes the lives of more and more workers. A technical writer at Intel, and a single father, describes his life:

Nominally, Intel has work hours, usually eight to five. . . . [But] life at Intel is intense . . . incredibly hard work. I'd get the kids up, give them breakfast, then I'd take off. Get there about seven in the morning. Usually I'd leave right at five. [He would come home to prepare dinner and eat with his daughters.] *Then I'd put them to bed at eight and come back to the office until about 1 A.M.*[46]

Devotion to market-oriented work now shapes the dominant cultural sense of self and others. Borsook argues that the devaluing of any form of life outside market-oriented work is part of an entrenched worldview. It strengthens a strongly libertarian philosophy that disdains government, celebrates individualism, sees the absolute ownership of private property as the basis of individual liberty, and describes economic life in terms of a hostile, evolutionary climate in which only the strong survive. Working long hours at paid employment has become the primary sign of responsible citizenship. The question "What do you do?" has only one meaning. Teenagers who work after school and on weekends are applauded for their self-discipline and commitment to "work." Proclaiming the importance of developing a work ethic, business interests that employ young workers and those who benefit from teenage spending typically resist attempts to restrict student hours in employment.[47] Low-income single mothers who do not "work" are by definition lazy.[48] We have become a people justified by paid "work," regardless of its quality, its compliance with the demands of justice; and we are suspicious of leisure.

But our families are stretched too far, now that *no one* should be at home. Arlie Hochschild comments, "while the mass media so often point to global competition as the major business story of the age, it is easy to miss the fact that corporate America's fiercest struggle has been with its local rival—the family."[49] What do worker flexibility, longer hours, and the new virtues required for success look like when experienced from the perspective of women's equality and family well-being? When time is money, what is the cost of family time, and who pays?

FAMILY-FRIENDLY CORPORATE TIME

"Family-friendly" policies is a term used to refer to those business practices that, in a concerted and coordinated way, help employees reach a healthy balance between work and family obligations.[50] The most common of these family-friendly business policies are aimed at providing employees with time flexibility. However, the warning raised by Andolsen in her examination of the "employability" contract must be heeded. "Flexibility" is also an employer's response to an increasingly fast moving and competitive marketplace. It is often a euphemism for brutal employment practices that permit businesses to renounce any stake in those persons providing them work.[51] Four types of time flexibility are generally considered family-friendly business policies: flextime, parental leave, part-time, and home-based work. Based on moral commitments to women's equality and families' well-being, these policies will be analyzed to uncover their underlying assumption upon which they are based: the form of the normative family, the appropriate beneficiaries of time flexibility, and the driving interest behind such policies.

Flextime

Flextime is the most commonly found policy in corporate America's attempt to be friendly to families. The Families and Work Institute's 1998 Business Work-Life Study (BWLS) of large companies found that 68 percent reported providing a traditional form of flextime: that is, employees may choose their starting and quitting times within a specified range of hours. However, only 24 percent of these large companies allowed employees to do so on a daily basis.[52] In a National Study of the Changing Workforce (NSCW), a survey of employees, 44 percent of employed parents with young children reported access to traditional flextime.[53] That is, they could choose their starting and quitting times within a range of hours. However, only 26 percent could do this as needed on a daily basis. While two-thirds of these employees said they could get time off during the day for family matters, over 50 percent said that they could not do so without losing pay or vacation time, or without making up some other excuse for needing to miss work.

These employees may be correctly assessing the deeply entrenched and negative managerial attitude toward employees who take time off for family issues that has already been documented. A survey of 106 employers with over one thousand employees each, conducted by the Washington Business Group on Health, found that 60 percent of the employers cited personal and family responsibilities as the fastest growing cause of employee absences. Yet, despite this evidence, 78 percent of these employers felt that the primary cause of employee absence was an *unmerited* attitude on the part of employees that they were entitled to time off.[54] Arlie Hochschild described the close attention paid to workers on one factory floor. Company data showed children's illnesses to be the cause of nine out of ten instances of work/family conflict for their employees. Nonetheless, managers placed a note in an employee's file on the first occasion of lateness for any reason, suspended the employee with unpaid days off for the second infraction, and after three such suspensions, fired the employee.[55]

I just got a written warning a couple of weeks ago because [my daughter] *was up all night and I was up all night with her, and . . . I couldn't go to work the next day and I got a written warning for missing too much time at work. . . .* [My sister's] *son was sick one day so she stayed down at my house . . . and when I came home she said that [her employer] had called down there and asked her to come up to the plant for a while, and they fired her.[56]*

Consequently, effective access to flexible hours is most often a perk for higher-paid employees. The NSCW survey found that lower-paid wage workers (those making less than $30,000 a year) were least likely to have this option. Only 1.6. percent of these workers were able to use flextime on a daily basis, compared to 42.4 percent of those making more that $45,000. Sixty percent of the lower-wage workers reported that they would lose a day's pay if it were necessary to stay home with a sick child (compared to 37 percent of those earning over $45,000). And low-wage workers were three times less likely to get company-sponsored tax breaks to help pay for childcare.[57]

Since most women workers are employed by smaller firms that typically offer fewer employee options than larger ones, even this data may be overstated. And, although black women tend to be employed full-time for more years than white women and are more likely to be employed in larger firms, they are also more likely to fill lower-wage jobs that do not have family-friendly benefits.[58] Simply looking closely at these aggregate statistics reveals the truthfulness of the conclusion reached by the editor of *Working Mother* magazine: "The vast majority of people in this country do not have flex time, do not get to go home early."[59]

> *When I started, the time was 7 A.M. It was understood when I started that my children go to the day care from 6:30 A.M. until 5:30 P.M., so that I could not possibly come in earlier than seven and stay past five. . . . Anyway, they changed the starting time to 6 A.M. and we have to stay until we are finished, even if it's after 5 P.M. You stay or you are terminated. . . . My neighbor is going to take the . . . kids at 5:30 in the morning so I can get to work at 6. That means we'll be getting up at 4:30. . . . The company really didn't give me any choice.[60]*

The expansion of flextime opportunities would certainly help workers balance their paid and unpaid work responsibilities. It might help two-parent families stretch out the length of time that at least one parent is not doing wage work. However, by definition, flextime does not decrease the increasing burden of hours spent at work. Flextime is primarily an operational decision to accommodate somewhat different starting and ending times for those employees whose work efficiency is not impaired by being at work earlier or later than the typically scheduled eight-hour day. As such it represents a very modest response to better-paid employees' family lives. It is still a response widely unavailable to average workers.

> *. . . the biggest pitfalls remain the same. Many employers want you to be very flexible with your schedule and work weekends and holidays. My babysitter*

doesn't work weekends or holidays. This makes it hard for me to find a job sometimes. Also, I have to work around my son's school schedule because I don't have any family/friends to help me do things. I really need a job that is flexible with me—one that allows me to take care of my family, as well as my work.[61]

Family and Medical Leave

Given the extent to which firms limit flextime use, employers' response to the idea of paternity leave should come as no surprise. Fifteen hundred CEOs and human resources directors from the nation's largest companies were asked what a reasonable length of time would be for paternity leave. Sixty-three percent said, "None."[62] One might suspect a connection between this view and the fact that, despite the wage work of most wives and mothers, the United States lags behind all other industrialized nations in addressing family/work concerns through public policies. This is not a reflection of the will of the people. Surveys consistently show strong support for paid parental leave and greater government involvement in helping families combine work and home responsibilities.[63] But business groups have consistently lobbied against any move in this direction. The Family and Medical Leave Act (FMLA) was debated by five congresses, passed by two, and vetoed twice by one president before it was finally signed into law early in 1993. Opponents argued that it was too costly and that it extended government reach into business matters best left to the market.

The final passage of the Act was a rare public acknowledgment of social responsibility for establishing the socioeconomic conditions that enable workers to care for dependents. FMLA gives workers the legal right to take up to twelve workweeks of unpaid leave within a twelve month period for any one of the following reasons: an employee gives birth to a child and needs to care for it; an employee has adopted a child or is receiving a foster-care child; an employee needs to care for a spouse, child, or parent who has a serious health condition; or, an employee has a serious health condition that makes him or her unable to perform their duties at work.

Congress listed a number of findings to justify the law. One was the recognition that families face an untenable choice between job security and parenting responsibilities. Another recognized that women bear the greater burden of family care, which can lead to discrimination against women in the workplace. Congress also argued that since any one of us may be severely impacted by a serious health condition of our own or of an immediate family member, society has an interest in providing citizens

support in those circumstances. Based on these findings, the purposes of
the Act were listed as follows: "to balance the demands of the workplace
with the needs of families, to promote the stability and economic security
of families, and to promote national interests in preserving family
integrity." Congress further stated that the Act was to promote the opportunity of equal employment for women and men.[64]

Given these purposes, the law's limitations are severe. First, family and
medical leave is unpaid. In a United Nations' survey of 152 countries, the
United States was one of only six countries that does not have a national
policy requiring paid maternity leave.[65] Since family and medical leave is
unpaid, one must wonder whom Congress had in mind. Certainly no one
who earns moderate- or low-income wages. Certainly not most single
mothers. Certainly not the families who would be removed from public
support and placed into low-wage work after the 1996 reform of welfare.
In 1996 the Commission on Leave Report to Congress confirmed that 64
percent of workers who need leave do not take it because they cannot
afford to take leave without pay. Of low-income workers who did take
some unpaid leave 21 percent had to turn to welfare for needed support.[66]
Maya is a lower-paid employee of a family-friendly corporation. At the
birth of her child, her employer's generous policy allowed her to take up to
six months of unpaid leave without losing her job. Unable to afford such
leave, Maya describes how she pieced together the care of her newborn:

> They say you can take as much time off as you want; I mean six months, you
> know. I couldn't afford to take that much time. I would have loved to, but you
> know, I got to work. So, I took a month off without pay. [My husband] took off
> the next month, and my mother-in-law took a month off from her work, and
> my mother had him for two weeks. Then after that I finally got him into the day
> care across the street.[67]

In addition to this severe limitation, the Act only applies to firms with
more than fifty employees. Workers in the private sector are eligible if they
have worked for at least a year and for at least 1,250 hours. Thus, just over
half of the work force, 55 percent, is actually covered by the Act.[68] In addition, an employer may deny leave to an employee who is part of the highest paid 10 percent in the business if granting leave would cause substantial
harm to the company. Moreover, the concept of family presumed by the
legislation is restricted to the most narrow of traditional nuclear-family
forms. It does not apply to caring for relatives who would be included in a
definition of extended family. It does not include leave to care for aunts,

uncles, grandparents, or even the parent of one's spouse. It does not include the members of same-sex families or cohabiting families.

Despite the rhetoric of family values, the United States is the last of the industrialized countries to adopt any form of family and medical leave. It has the dubious distinction of being the only industrialized country to provide a legal right to *unpaid* leave for only *half* of its work force.[69] Part of the explanation for this aberration lies in the power of conservative religious discourse and its defense of the nineteenth century's partnership between patriarchal families and the wage-labor basis of capitalism.[70] Another part lies in the libertarian, antigovernment ideology that permeates the glamorous world of high-tech industry and its current heroes.[71] As *Time* reports in an on-line review of its Person of the Year choices: "Business leaders like Ted Turner and Jeff Bezos reigned supreme in the booming 90s. . . ."[72]

However, the Act itself pointedly expressed the one concern that ultimately overrode all others: that the purposes of the Act must be accomplished in a manner "that accommodates the legitimate interests of employers."[73] Whatever interests the U.S. Congress may believe it has in preserving family integrity by promoting the stability and economic security of families or in promoting gender equality, these concerns must accommodate the demands for efficiency in business in a neoliberal political economy. Heilbroner refers to such reasoning as the "de-moralization of economic activity."[74] The privatization of economic interests effectively rules out of bounds a prior discussion of social values and social results. The benefits of material gain, or at least the promise of material gain, particularly as they get measured with such abstracted statistics as GDP, per capita income, corporate profits, and stock prices, seem to outweigh any concern for advancing the moral quality of society by including equality for women and the well-being of families.

> *I have always had a job, even during my pregnancy, being sick and everything. But now it's hard with a child and [with him] having asthma. It's extra rough. I can get a job, and everything can be going along fine for a month or so, and then he gets sick. And then it's like, "Oh, God, what should I do? Should I stay here with him, or should I try to go to work?" If I go to work and he has an attack, they are going to call me, and then if I'm at work, I'm not supposed to leave post. So that's rough. . . . So I'm not really worried about finding a job, because I know I can get one. It's the challenge of keeping it, with my son, and not letting the employer think I'm a person who doesn't want to work.[75]*

Part-Time Work

The growth in employment hours demanded by the new economy, the lack of actual flexibility in full-time work hours, and the inaccessibility of even the most traditional form of flextime to the lower-wage workers who need it the most, raise the option of part-time work. Is part-time work a solution for families? Can families achieve gender equality and economic stability even at a modest middle-income standard through part-time work?

To answer those questions, one needs to keep in mind that, for middle- and low-income families, the movement of wives and mothers into wage work in the last three decades was a response to the threatened economic well-being of their families. Behind the veneer of prosperity in the 1980s and 1990s, there was long-term stagnation in wages and the addition of more hours to employed work in order to stay even. Consequently, under current economic conditions and trends, solving the imbalance between employed and family time by reducing full-time jobs to part-time jobs, while maintaining a middle-income standard of living, would be impossible for most families. It would be impossible for the 60 percent of black, married, dual-full-time-earner couples and the 37 percent of white, dual-full-time-earner couples who now have a middle level of income.[76] It would be impossible for those married couples whose annual income is below $25,000. (18.5 percent of poor families are families with two adults and children under eighteen.)[77] It would be impossible for the 40 percent of American households whose total yearly income is $39,300 or less.

Who are these workers? Some of them are the employees of the new dot.coms that symbolize the new economy. Amazon.com's college-educated customer-service representatives earned $10 (tier I) and $11 (tier II) an hour in the fall of 2000. Only by working the mandatory ten hours of overtime each week did a worker raise his or her annual income above $25,000.[78] A thirty-hour week would also be impossible for the 12.9 million workers who earn less than $6.65 an hour.[79] In 1997, former welfare recipients who were now working earned a median hourly wage of $6.61— slightly over $10,000 annually for full-time work.[80] It would be impossible for the restaurant workers, security guards, daycare workers, and attendants for the elderly—that is, it would be impossible for the service employees who fill the boom in low-income jobs.[81] It would be impossible for migrant workers picking tomatoes in Florida, or lettuce in California, or cherries in Michigan.

While not possible in the current economic system for most families, a part-time worker solution may be more applicable for high-income families, particularly those in which both spouses have achieved positions at high levels of compensation. Perhaps those in the top earning 20 percent of U.S. families, earning over $64,900 a year, could afford to reduce consumption and hours of paid work. For example, the size of the average home in the United States today is 53 percent larger than it was in 1970 even though the average family is 15 percent smaller. The average size of newly constructed homes is almost 2,500 square feet because the children of these families are not expected to share a bedroom and each spouse is expected to have a room of one's own, by whatever name. What makes this home "average," however, are the even larger homes, the McMansions of 5,000 square feet or more, which are sustaining home construction in a time of economic slowdown.[82] Overworking to support overconsumption *is* a moral issue for some.

However, the debate over the so-called mommy track highlighted the problems of higher-paid women who choose to reduce their work hours.[83] A middle-manager in a large family-friendly company described the actual climate for women managers.

> *Old-time management in the company still have an old mind-set about women and work and family. And from what I've noticed the women who generally get to the top are the women who don't have the children. You have to sacrifice something to get there. Either you sacrifice your children if you have them, or the ones who don't have the children give that further commitment, and so I think the people who are at the top have different attitudes toward [their workers] taking [leave] time.[84]*

The impact of the new economy, coupled with pervasive traditional gender expectations, has little patience with family time. However, it has created *some* part-time work as a way of retaining skilled and professional workers who do not want to work full-time—an option typically stigmatized as a gender-specific response for upper-income women who can afford this choice.[85] In fact, few professionals and managers are employed part-time. Those who are are most likely to be married, white women, with children, whose husbands have high salaries.[86]

A study of part-time lawyers in New York is illustrative. The authors report that while 92 percent of law offices have part-time policies, just 2.6 percent of lawyers work part-time—and almost all of them are women responding to family needs.[87] The most obvious cost of part-time work for these women was reduced income for reduced hours. Presumably this was a cost these women were willing to incur because they were all married to high-income-earning professional husbands. However, the authors also discovered significant hidden costs to part-time professionals: the experience of both disapproval and envy from colleagues, the loss of more demanding assignments, lack of promotion, less access to office and support resources, being perceived as less committed to work and as less competent, less ability to network with colleagues and clients, and more likelihood of being blamed for failures.

An American Bar Association survey found that 96 percent of law associates and 89 percent of law partners believed that a willingness to work long hours was an important factor in consideration for promotion.[88] Choosing to work part-time professionally is likely to have similar results for men as well as women. But it is women who, in fact, make this "choice": 26 to 29 percent of married women professionals and managers with children work part-time, but only 1 to 2 percent of professional and managerial men do.[89] This may help explain the results of an interesting survey that found that firms with the best family-friendly policies actually have the worst records for advancing women.[90] There is, then, another cost to part-time work for professional people. It is a cost of competence, of one's capacity to be excellent in one's field. This is a cost that women in the academy know well. The very intensive stages of completing the dissertation, job placement, research and publication that are necessary for gaining and retaining a position come at the beginning of one's career and coincide with decisions about marriage and childbearing. Virginia Valian has documented the long-lasting impact on women's academic careers of even small amounts of unequal dedication, actual or perceived.[91]

But most women workers are not better-paid professionals. Most women work in the secondary labor market characterized by jobs with "low wages, few or no benefits, little opportunity for advancement, and unstable employment."[92] These are also the kind of jobs most women in part-time work hold.[93] Part-time work at this level is an employer's strategy to increase staff flexibility and to cut even further costs in industries that typically rely on a low-skill and low-cost work force (retail, grocery, insurance, etc.). But because of dependent-care responsibilities and limited work options, women are more likely than men to choose part-time work.[94] White women are more likely than women of other racial/ethnic minorities to engage in part-time work: 28.3 percent of white women in the labor force work part-time compared to 18.5 percent of black women workers.[95] Minority workers are more likely to work in part-time jobs involuntarily.[96]

Furthermore, women make up the majority of those workers who combine several part-time jobs to total more than thirty-five hours of work a week.[97] One reason for this may be the gap between wages that disqualify one from receiving public subsidies and the actual income a family needs to meet the "self-sufficiency standard," a measure of how much money a working family requires to actually meet their basic needs in the community where they live. Typically, the self-sufficiency standard falls between 50 percent and 80 percent of the area's median income. It is always well above the federal poverty guideline.[98] A study of five boroughs in New York found that to meet the bare necessities in those boroughs, a family would need two to five times more than indicated by federal poverty levels. In the Bronx, to make ends meet, one mother combined a full-time job as an administrative assistant paying $24,000 with a part-time job paying $10 an hour—until her two teenagers began to have problems. Spending time with them caused her to lose her full-time job. Now she works nightshifts and weekends, often with mandatory overtime, and earns $22,000. But, she says, *"I'll be out for a second job soon, because $22,000 is just not enough."* For this mother and her children to be self-sufficient in the Bronx, the "self-sufficiency standard" estimates that she will need to earn $38,000 annually.[99]

Part-time work exacts a high price from workers in low- and moderate-income families. They pay not only the immediate economic price of lower wages per hour and less hours; they also have less access to health insurance, sick and family leave, and unemployment and disability insurance. They face the long-term economic consequences related to inadequate Social Security benefits and no employer-sponsored pensions. They receive little or no training, face unexpected job loses, and are less likely to be unionized. In the time-and-wages hierarchy of the wage-labor system, part-time work may be a workable strategy for some highly skilled and high-income workers. For most women who work part-time, it is a strategy for survival in the crisis of balancing income needs and other family needs. It is a risky strategy. At neither end of the economic spectrum does part-time work serve the goal of gender justice. At the low end, it denies access to the goal of family well-being.

I've been on county assistance since I was pregnant. . . . I waitress. I've always waitressed. . . . I work three days a week . . . my sister baby-sits for me . . . the money gets tight. . . . The only reason I don't work full-time is that she needs to know I am here, because he isn't here. She needs to know she has me to depend on. If she needs me, I am here. But I don't want to be a waitress all my life.[100]

To make part-time work a possibility for most American families will require a major transformation in the economic system. It will require challenging the new economy's demand for more and more flexibility, its insistence that all time is money. It will require a return to what now seem like radical visions from the 1960s: full-time work defined as thirty to thirty-five hours a week and *one* full-time job paying a living wage for a family.

> *I was out looking up and down Main Street for a job. Filled out* [an] *application and got hired the next day. Started at $6 per hour. After two months,* [I] *became a shift supervisor and got $8 per hour.* [The job] *has high turnover and it causes me to have to work more shifts.* [It] *causes stress and this comes home. With working different shifts, I'm tired when I get home. My husband works second shift and I have to take care of the kids by myself. The long hours are tough and cuts down on the amount of fun time I get with my kids. I enjoy my job and working there.*[101]

Home Production

Work at home has always been a part of industrialized capitalism. It is also a part of post-industrial capitalism. In its new incarnation, working-at-home is celebrated as a good solution for mothers as well as a friendly corporate response to family needs. An ethical evaluation of work at home needs to keep in mind that there are three distinct types of home workers: employees who do some work at home; small business owners who work from their homes; and piece workers who work under contracts at home. In the following discussion we need to determine whether these forms of work serve the values of gender equality and family well-being.

Some employees work both at home and at the office. As employees, they maintain the advantages of salaried or hourly wages, with benefits. For some of these home workers, new technologies in telecommunications allow employed work to follow them into the home and into all family activities—a blessing and a curse. Everyone is lured by the images of an up-scale mother who decides to skip the office in order to teleconference from the beach, e-mail from the den, and answer clients' inquiries while stirring homemade soup . . . happy children at her feet. According to the International Telework Association and Council, about 12 percent of the work force now works at home one or more days a week.[102] For some, it provides helpful flexibility of time and space. As some studies have shown, employees experience less stress and less work/life time imbalance when they have some control over their schedules even though the workload is not reduced.[103] Yet, this flexibility has two negative consequences.

First, flexible location may appear to free employees for family time; but, in fact, that is not its intent. Its intent is to keep employed work on schedule despite family responsibilities. It allows the work of salaried, white-collar, professional people to penetrate the family more completely. Market-oriented work expands both spatially and temporally into family life. Offices are replicated at home and in cars. No one escapes the beeper, home fax machine, scanners, copiers, and e-mail. Commuting time has been converted to time for returning business calls. As one company president remarked, "If someone wants to stop at 2 P.M. to take their child to a soccer game, as long as they take a cell phone or call in every hour and a half for their messages, that's fine."[104] Fraser calls this phenomenon "job spill." She writes that it is "like an oil spill. . . ."

> . . . imagine job tasks seeping from the office to the home in much the same way as oil can invade a body of water and a beach. The seepage is just as difficult to block. And it's the dirty secret behind many a corporation's thriving bottom line.[105]

Job spill seeps into every second of business trips and vacation travel. Planes, airports, hotel rooms, and poolsides come furnished with computer jacks, internet kiosks, faxes, and copiers. New aquatic gadgets include water-resistant cordless phones and a floating lounge chair designed for use with a laptop. Some companies, AOL, for example, actually announce "e-mail-free" weekends as special occasions when employees are officially relieved of the necessity to check their e-mail. A CFO described life with the new technology in communications:

> We've all got the cell phones, the beepers, the laptops. I bring mine back and forth between my home and office every day. Everybody does it—you feel like you always need to be accessible. Even when you're on vacation, you've got to be accessible. You've got to be prepared to check in all the time. All those pieces of equipment are a big reason we're working harder.[106]

Research supports personal testimony. Forty-one percent of those who own cell phones have used them to call the office while on vacation; 34 percent have checked their office answering machine or voice-mail while on vacation; 53 percent of those with beepers have been beeped by the office while on vacation.[107] Yet, this is time typically not counted as market-oriented time. It is time-on-the-job in which the lack of rules provides no final whistle-blast to end the workday. Technology brings more market-oriented work demands, brings them faster, and creates the expectation that they will be answered quickly, efficiently, and tirelessly. Technology is not the real culprit. Job spill affects even low-skill workers. The real culprit is the quickening pace of work for everyone. In the context of the time demands of the new economy, every moment and every place is *worked*.

> *I put in a lot of hours at my job. I work Monday-Friday from 9–4:30, then I go home and work at least every night [for] five hours on opening mail for my company. I work for a mail order company. By me bringing work home at night I am able to spend very little time with my four children. On weekends, I spend as much as eight to eleven hours opening mail, so I don't get to spend as much time with my family as I would like to.*[108]

A second negative consequence may make many employees reluctant to use these technologies, even when it might be to the advantage of family life. As studies of part-time work show, lack of visibility *in* the office is a significant detriment to career advancement for professional women. The use of flexible location options may very well increase women's disadvantages as long as business continues to operate on the assumption that family concerns are unfortunate baggage that some employees (women) carry. In fact, in the face of growing competition, U.S. companies have established new models of organizing work to increase productivity: total quality management, empowerment, self-managed teams, and reduced levels of mid-management. The result, according to Lotte Bailyn, is the need for greater employee participation *at* work. More time and more energy is expected for an intensified, self-directed, commitment to a project.[109] Thus, while advanced telecommunication equipment makes transporting service and information-related work into the home possible, the re-organization of work and management in the new economy still measures commitment by the office clock.

However, this picture of wired professionals does not describe most home workers and their home-based employment. A more accurate picture is that of the two other forms of home work: the self-employed home worker who has no consistent work space elsewhere and regularly works at home for income; and what I call the "invisible employee" home worker.

The self-employed home worker is typically motivated to work at home because of a perceived lack of other employment opportunities, or in response to entrepreneurial hopes, or to achieve a sense of more personal freedom and responsibility.[110] Many of those interviewed in a large, nine-state study turned to work at home because of the recession of the early 1980s. Starting a home-based business was typically a strategy to supplement the wages of another family member who was employed outside the home. These home workers were responsible for all the activities related to running a business: advertising, production, accounting, and so forth. Most home business owners provided some sort of service, such as childcare, mechanical or small appliance repairs, real estate sales, or personal services. Most of the home business owners worked over forty hours a week, experienced more income instability than wage workers, and typically had few benefits such as pensions and health insurance.

Gender makes a significant difference among home business owners. Because of the gendered division of labor, gender assumptions shape the types of home work women and men do and, therefore, the economic outcomes. Men tend to be self-employed as contractors, mechanics, and workers in profession–technical fields, earning an average of $24,648 annually. Women generally provide services (daycare, piano lessons), do clerical work, or make crafts. They average $8,614 annually. Accommodating family responsibilities while earning some income is a major factor for women who choose work at home. Most mothers in this study integrated the care of their own children with their home work activities, but the success of this strategy depended upon the type of work being done. As other studies indicate, many mothers do home work while their children are being cared for by others, are asleep, or at school. Moreover, women experience more interruptions to both family time and market-oriented time than do men. The presence of children is shown to have a negative impact on women's annual earnings but not on men's. There is, in fact, no evidence that women experience less work/family conflict when they engage in home-based, market-oriented work.[111]

Home workers who own their own business must also be distinguished from the low-income women (and often their families) who work as wage or piece-rate earners. These are the home workers I have called "invisible employees." Barbara Paleczny refers to them as unprotected laborers— "without a formal contract or benefits, expected to perform with limited control and autonomy, and without adequate compensation."[112] For these workers, home work looks quite different from either the high-tech telecommuter or the home business owner. They participate in a process of work decentralization that is global. Referred to as a "satellite factory system" or "front room factories," this work is part of a hierarchically structured, subcontracting system in which small-scale, family-controlled units "polish, assemble, pack and package."[113] They work for small, peripheral industries with which larger companies have contracted-out assembly or clerical functions in order to reduce labor and overhead costs. The smaller firms absorb the pressures of competition for the larger ones and do so successfully through the use of these contingent workers. These home workers are dependent upon firms to provide them with work. They do not receive the benefits of regular employees, are usually paid on a per-piece basis, and in the United States typically earn only 76 percent of comparable at-work workers.[114]

In Toronto, invisible employees of the garment industry, most of whom are immigrant women, make less than half of what they made when doing the same work in the factory setting.[115] Here, restructuring of the garment industry has meant the closing of factories and an increase in small subcontracting shops that mete out piecework to home workers in order to compete with women garment workers in Thailand, Honduras, El Salvador, Poland, and elsewhere. Most of the Toronto home workers do not make minimum wages. Electronic home workers in rural, central New York rarely make minimum wage. As one veteran of eleven years remarked, *"If you were very fast, you could almost make minimum wage, but mostly you would come up short of the minimum."*[116] Despite working at home, time for these home workers is not their own. The workload fluctuates according to the demands of the subcontractor. In busy seasons the average number of hours worked per week by the garment workers in Toronto was seventy hours, with no overtime pay. Yet, in slow seasons, hours could be reduced to as little as sixteen a week.

Gender myths, coupled now with the ideology of neoliberal capitalism, serve to make the realities of these workers invisible. It is the task of Christian ethics to examine the myths and the structures of dis-information that support exploitation. One myth exploits the romantic image of women combining family work with income-producing work. This myth assumes that family work is not work; that it takes up little time and effort and is easily rearranged to suit the time needed for income-producing home work. In the rosy hue cast by the mere mention of "family," the capacity of family members to absorb all forms of economic instability is assumed. Reality is mystified.

Contrary to the myths, these invisible employees do not escape the juggling act of balancing work and family time. They work early; they work late; they work when husbands and other relatives are available to watch the children. And often children and spouses help with the work by folding and cutting threads, picking up more work and delivering finished products—all without pay. The Toronto garment workers emphasized the stress of trying to finish income-producing work quickly while family members expected the attention of a wife/mother who is at home. The noise of the machines and the appropriation of limited household space for home work further increased family stress. The invisible employee works at home because of few good employment or childcare options.[117] Like her nineteenth-century counterparts, her work reveals the cost to families of the process of capital accumulation. She does factory work at home for less money and no benefits because family survival requires it. As Paleczny reports,

> Most women extended their work day deep into the night and found that it took a toll on their relationships with their husbands and their children. Furthermore, they preferred working at home only to not working for income at all.[118]

A second myth celebrates the freedom of home workers. Someone's freedom is being advanced, but it is not the home worker's. The use of invisible employees has expanded into many types of work: auto- and electrical-parts assembly, telemarketing and taking phone orders, stuffing envelopes, and even food preparation. By considering the home worker as self-employed, governments permit and business firms enjoy freedom from all sorts of regulations related to working conditions, health and safety standards, wages, benefits, sick leave, child labor, and, of course, family-friendly policies. The use of home workers frees companies from direct and indirect labor costs. It creates more lowest-cost competition that destabilizes the wage gains and employment protections of on-site workers doing the same work. Even in economically overdeveloped nations, like the United States and Canada, home working serves to integrate a national industry into competitive, global trading zones. National industries can compete for low-wage work in quick-response time without leaving the country. Jobs are kept, wages are earned, and corporate profits are made. According to the myths of postindustrial capitalism, worker autonomy has been increased and efficiency in the production of socially needed goods has been accomplished in a win–win situation. Everyone's freedom has been enhanced. All this, and in addition, work/family conflict has been reduced.

The reality is quite different.

> Ming-Zhen sews a woman's jacket in one hour and earns $4.15. She receives no compensation for training time when new styles arrive. She must teach

herself the new design. The jacket is sold at Eaton's for $275 to $375. Poi-Yee makes $5 for sewing a dress in one hour, but she has had to buy the sewing machine and cover all operating costs such as hydro and heat. The dress is sold for $150 to $200 at a high-end boutique. A contractor often delivers work on Friday to Yen, who must complete it by Monday morning. She must care for her children while she sews at least ten hours a day all weekend.[119]

The global economics of the garment industry provide an example of how the daily lives of ordinary people are impacted by decisions being made in distant places by people fully unaccountable to the outcomes of their economic rationality. Today, a centralized level of large retailers control production of garments as well as the cost. Retailers have the power to set the price they will pay to the lower level of large super-label manufacturers, while following business practices that place more and more market risk upon the manufacturers and their subcontractors. Retailers set production demands in terms of packaging, labeling, and pre-pricing, shipment accuracy, time schedules, and quantities. The Hudson's Bay Company uses an electronic data exchange system for just-in-time production that allows it to order specific stock without itself accumulating inventory. (This is the same type of system introduced by Wal-Mart into the United States.) The manufacturer has to cover this additional risk by reducing its overhead. The manufacturer (such as Liz Claiborne, Jones New York) designs the garment and buys the material, but to reduce overhead typically contracts out the cutting and assembly jobs. New designs may be developed, or new styles, or new colors, within a matter of weeks. A quick-response process has cut the turnaround time between design and arrival at stores from twelve months to less than three weeks. Subcontractors, "jobbers," then subcontract the cutting and sewing to smaller factories, to sweatshops, that contract with the home worker. The more labor-intensive the job, the more it is sent to the lowest-wage workers wherever they are. At the bottom of the pyramid, workers around the world scramble to fill shortfalls in production, to retrain for new designs, to accept part-time work, wage concessions, and nonstandard working time. Yet, at the top of the pyramid, retailers are "free" to mark-up the garments—typically 100 to 200 percent. The basic logic of capitalism today is the same as it was a century ago.[120]

Yet, the neoliberal language of freedom and autonomy banishes from view exploitative wages and working conditions. They become conditions of "freedom," expressions of "autonomy," and new "opportunities." The language of neoliberalism hides the actual demands of work done to exacting specifications in quantities and time periods imposed by the supplier.

The invisible employee is "free" when free means unprotected. The unprotected laborer at the bottom of a global pyramid is a tool in the strategy of reducing the cost of labor and production by achieving the ultimate in labor flexibility. Essentially, the risk involved in maintaining a labor force through business cycles is absorbed by the home worker herself and her family as she purchases her own equipment, stores materials and finished products, wrestles with her own allergies to fabrics and chemicals, pays for her own lighting, and deals with the lack of ventilation, sore muscles, back problems, and migraine headaches. She works and gets paid by the piece, or, as demand slackens, she does not work and does not get paid. Freedom and opportunity, without the power to effect the decisions that impact one's life, are cynical names for exploitation.

Time is money. Now all time and everyone's time is money. In the squeeze between spending time to earn very needed income and spending time at home with children or others needing care, middle-income women and families manage by buying time. Good families buy the products and services that they no longer have time to do in the new economy. They are bought from economically poorer women whose lives reveal a deeper truth: at the bottom of the hierarchy of well-being, families need time—and money.

NOTES

1. Edward Wong, "A Stinging Office Memo Boomerangs," *New York Times*, 5 April 2001: C1, C13.

2. Benjamin Franklin, *The Autobiography of Benjamin Franklin* (New York: Washington Square Press, 1955), 103, cited in Michael Novak, *The Spirit of Democratic Capitalism* (Lanham, Md.: Madison Books, 1982, 1991), 97.

3. Cited in Juliet Schor, *The Overworked American: The Unexpected Decline of Leisure* (New York: Basic Books, 1991), 4.

4. Martin Carnoy, *Sustaining the New Economy: Work, Family, and Community in the Information Age* (New York: Russell Sage Foundation, 2000), 56.

5. Edmund L. Andrews, "As American Economy Slows, Europeans Suddenly Feel Flush," *New York Times*, 2 February 2001: A1, C2. On the same page, growing homelessness in Japan was attributed to a broken system of employee protections. A Japanese official states, "These people have become economic refugees, and the basic problem is that when the economy is bad, there is no work, and people without work will eventually become homeless." Howard W. French, "Brooding Over

Its Homeless, Japan Sees a Broken System," *New York Times*, 2 February 2001: A1, A10.

6. Edmund L. Andrews, "Germany Weighs Overhaul of 'Consensus' Capitalism, *New York Times,* 14 February 2001: W1, W7. These laws require companies with at least 301 workers to give workers' representatives a third of the seats on their supervisory boards. Medium and large companies must also have workers' councils that have the legal right to veto such management decisions as hiring and firing workers, to be informed of plans to downsize, to approve compensation packages for dismissed employees, and so forth. When companies want to impose layoffs, they have to develop plans to protect the jobs of older workers and of people responsible for supporting families. Edmund L. Andrews, "Europe Toughens Up on Job Cuts," *New York Times*, 1 December 2001: C1, C3.

7. Louis Uchitelle, "Pink Slip? Now, It's All in a Day's Work," *New York Times*, 5 August 2001: BU1, 11.

8. Jennifer Lee, "Discarded Dreams of Dot-Com Rejects," *New York Times*, 21 February 2001: C1, C8.

9. Jonathan D. Glater, "For Last Paycheck, More Workers Cede Their Right to Sue," *New York Times*, 24 February 2001: A1, B16.

10. Jane Slaughter, "Overtime Out: Nurses Strike to End Dangerously Long Shifts," *In These Times*, 10 February 2001: 10–11.

11. Mark Leibovich, "Not All Smiles Inside Amazon.com," *The Washington Post*, 25 November 1999; available at http://seattletimes.nwsource.com/news/technology/html98/amaz_19991125.html. Washington Alliance of Technology Workers, "Holiday in Amazonia," *Industry News*, 21 December 1998; available at www.washtech.org//roundup/news/amazon.html.

12. Steven Greenhouse, "Phone Workers Fight for Place in Wireless Era," *New York Times*, 31 July 2000: A1, A12.

13. Mindy Fried, *Taking Time: Parental Leave Policy and Corporate Culture* (Philadelphia: Temple University Press, 1998), 30.

14. Ibid., 39.

15. Schor, *The Overworked American*, 30–32.

16. For the argument that Americans have gained in leisure time since the 1960s, see John P. Robinson, Geoffrey Godbey, Anne Jacobson, *Time for Life: The Surprising Way Americans Use Their Time* (State College: Pennsylvania State University Press, 1999). For Schor's response to similar arguments, see Appendix B in *The Overworked American*, 168–69.

17. David Leonhardt, "Lingering Job Worries Amid a Sea of Plenty," *New York Times,* 29 August 2000: C1, C5.

18. Steven Greenhouse, "Report Shows Americans Have More 'Labor Days.'" *New York Times*, 1 September 2001: A6. See also Steven Greenhouse, "So Much Work, So Little Time," *New York Times*, 5 September 1999: 1WK, 4WK. Europeans' longer vacation times, four to six weeks, are protected by legislation. The higher productivity rate of the United States is tied to more hours, not to greater productivity per worker per hour.

19. Louis Uchitelle, "At the Desk, Off the Clock and Below Statistical Radar," *New York Times*, 18 July 1999: BU 4; Stephen S. Roach, "Working Better or Just Harder," *New York Times*, 14 February 2000: A27. Roach is chief economist for Morgan Stanley Dean Witter.

20. Institute for Women's Policy Research, *Network News* 8, no. 2 (June 1999): 1.

21. David H. Ciscel, David C. Sharp, and Julia A. Heath, "Family Work Trends and Practices: 1971 to 1991," *Journal of Family and Economic Issues* 21, no. 1 (Spring 2000): 27–28, 35; Jill Andresky Fraser, *White-Collar Sweatshop: The Deterioration of Work and Its Rewards in Corporate America* (New York: W. W. Norton, 2001), 119–20.

22. Mary Williams Walsh, "Reversing Decades-Long Trend, Americans Retiring Later in Life," *New York Times*, 26 February 2001: A1, A13. A report from the National Bureau of Economic Research shows that "the average American at retirement has total financial assets of about $40,000, including company retirement plans and personal savings. If you exclude company retirement plans, the figure drops to $13,000." Social Security is the primary source of retirement income for most of the population. See Hal R. Varian, "Economic Scene: With privatization, market risks could put a hole in the Social Security safety net," *New York Times*, 31 May 2001: C2.

23. John O'Neil and Marjorie Connelly, "As Savings Go Up, Worries Go Down (A Little)," *New York Times*, 21 March 2001: C1, C10. In another survey, only 22 percent of all workers surveyed said that they were "very confident" that they "will have enough money to live comfortably in retirement." Riva D. Atlas, "Why Juan Won't Save," *New York Times*, 20 June 2001: C1.

24. See Louis Uchitelle, "Workers Find Retirement Is Receding Toward 70," *New York Times*, 3 February 2002: BU 4; Jill Andresky Fraser. *White-Collar Sweatshop*, 58–74.

25. Ibid. While 401(k)s were touted as placing workers in the same market that has benefited the wealthy, their CEOs and CFOs, the reality is that corporate management has access to information, much greater freedom to diversify their savings, and, often, company-financed pension plans. Consequently, Uchitelle argues, workers have been ushered into an area of risk without the protections that the wealthy have to cope with market downturns. Louis Uchitelle, "The Rich Are Different. They Know When to Leave," *New York Times*, 20 January 2002: WK 1, 5.

26. Novak, *Spirit of Democratic Capitalism*, 101.

27. Paulina Borsook, *Cyberselfish: A Critical Romp through the Terribly Libertarian Culture of High Tech* (New York: Public Affairs, 2000), 41.

28. Fraser, *White-Collar Sweatshop*, 18–19.

29. Uchitelle, "At the Desk," BU 4; Roach, "Working Better," A27.

30. Yet, fewer than 30 percent of those who file for unemployment insurance receive it, and only 31 percent of unemployed women receive benefits compared to 37 percent of unemployed men. Unemployment insurance typically excludes people who work part-time, those recently hired into low-wage work (such as

recent welfare recipients), those who quit their jobs (perhaps to care for a sick relative), and those who refuse a new shift or a geographical move for family reasons. Part-time workers pay unemployment insurance tax while working but do not receive unemployment benefits in most states. David Leonhardt, "Out of Work, and out of the Benefits Loop," *New York Times*, 17 October 2001: C1, C13; Robert B. Reich, "Lost Jobs, Ragged Safety New," *New York Times*, 12 November 2001: A23; Heidi Hartmann, "Placing Women First and Center: New Family and Economic Realities," Press Conference Comments, 2 November 2001, available at www.iwpr.org/comments.

31. Frederick F. Reichheld, "Lead for Loyalty," *Harvard Business Review* (July/August 2000); available at www.hbsp.harvard.edu/products/hbr.

32. Paul Osterman, cited in Louis Uchitelle, "These Days Layoffs Compete with Loyalty," *New York Times*, 19 August 2001: BU 4.

33. Laurence J. Stybel and Maryanne Peabody, "The Right Way to be Fired," *Harvard Business Review* (July/August 2000); available at www.hbsp.harvard.edu/products/hbr. According to a Gallup survey conducted in 1999 with two million employees at seven hundred companies, 56 percent of employees believe that their company does not care about them or their careers, and 55 percent said that they have no strong loyalty to their company. Amy Zipkin, "The Wisdom of Thoughtfulness: In Tight Labor Market, Bosses Find Value in Being Nice," *New York Times*, 31 May 2000: C1, C10.

34. Andrew S. Grove, *Only the Paranoid Survive: How to Exploit the Crisis Points That Challenge Every Company and Career* (New York: Currency, Doubleday, 1996), 6, cited in Jill Andresky Fraser, *White-Collar Sweatshop*, 139. Intel changed the terms of its employment contract from "for cause" to "at will" in the early 1990s.

35. Carnoy, *Sustaining the New Economy*, 56–57. For another celebration of the free, unfettered worker, see Daniel H. Pink, *Free Agent Nation: How America's New Independent Workers Are Transforming the Way We Live* (New York: Warner Business Books, 2001).

36. Carnoy, *Sustaining the New Economy*, 5.

37. Ibid., 1. Carnoy is assuming jobs that do in fact teach new skills. However, similar expectations of employee flexibility for the sake of efficiency are imposed upon service sector workers whose jobs provide no opportunity for skill enhancement. These workers are also expected to avoid contact and lasting relationships with fellow employees. Their need to feel a sense of relationship is manipulated toward their employer. See Barbara Ehrenreich, *Nickel and Dimed: On (Not) Getting By in America* (New York: Metropolitan Books, 2001).

38. Andrea G. Eisenberg, Managing Principal of Right Management Consultants, quoted in Uchitelle, "Pink Slip?": BU 11.

39. Margaret K. Nelson and Joan Smith, *Working Hard and Making Do: Surviving in Small Town America* (Berkeley: University of California Press, 1999), 158.

40. Thomas J. Cottle, *Hardest Times: The Trauma of Long Term Unemployment*

(Westport, Conn.: Praeger, 2000). For the corporate spin on layoffs, see Fraser, *White-Collar Sweatshop*, chap. 9; David Leonhardt, "Yes, Layoffs Still Hurt, Even During Good Times," *New York Times*, 17 May 2001: BU 4.

41. Fraser, *White-Collar Sweatshop*, 53–57.

42. Ibid., 156.

43. Radcliffe Public Policy Center, *Life's Work: Generational Attitudes toward Work and Life Integration*, available at www.radcliffe.edu/pibpol. See summary in *The National Report on Work and Family*, 2000 Business Publishers, Inc., 13, no. 10 (16 May 2000): 81–82.

44. Schor, *The Overworked American*, 152; Jill Andresky Fraser, *White-Collar Sweatshop*. Of course, if competition demands it, firms may indeed cut hours. An interesting example occurred when the Charles Schwab Corporation, a brokerage firm, ordered half of its employees to *not* show up on three of the following five Fridays. The employees were expected to either use vacation time or unpaid leave. Either way the corporation wanted to reduce its compensation costs by $9 to $15 million in order to bolster its reported earnings for the quarter. Patrick McGeehan, "Schwab Tells Some Workers to Stay Home," *New York Times*, 31 January 2001: C1, C2.

45. Rosalind C. Barnett and Caryl Rivers, *She Works He Works: How Two-Income Families Are Happier, Healthier, and Better-Off* (San Francisco: HarperSanFrancisco, 1996), 65.

46. Fraser, *White-Collar Sweatshop*, 21–22.

47. Of U.S. high school seniors 55 percent work three or more hours on a regular school day, compared to an 18 percent average for other nations. Negative effects seem to be associated with working more than fifteen hours a week: lower grades, absenteeism from school, alcohol and drug use, and the selection of less demanding courses. Richard Rothstein, "When After-School Jobs Lead to Poor Performance in School," *New York Times*, 31 October 2001: A14.

48. See Michael B. Katz, *The Undeserving Poor: From the War on Poverty to the War on Welfare* (New York: Pantheon Books, 1989), esp. chaps. 1 and 4 for an account of how poverty has been transformed from an economic problem to a problem of morality and culture.

49. Arlie Russell Hochschild, *The Time Bind: When Work Becomes Home and Home Becomes Work* (New York: Metropolitan Books, 1997), 203–4.

50. For an interesting study of what promotes a family-friendly management, see Steven Wood, "Family-friendly Management: Testing the Various Perspectives," *National Institute Economic Review* 168 (April 1999): 99–116.

51. Barbara Hilkert Andolsen, *The New Job Contract: Economic Justice in an Age of Insecurity* (Cleveland: Pilgrim Press, 1998), 24.

52. Ellen Galinsky and James T. Bond, "The 1998 Business Work-Life Study: Executive Summary," The Family and Work Institute, www.familiesandwork.org.

53. James T. Bond, Ellen Galinsky, Jennifer E. Swanberg, *The 1997 National Study of the Changing Workforce* (New York: Families and Work Institute, 1998),

98–99. See also Rima Shore, "Ahead of the Curve: Why America's Leading Employers are Addressing the Needs of New and Expectant Parents," Families and Work Institute, executive summary available at www.familiesandwork.org/summary/curve.pdf.

54. "Survey Finds Employers Can Reduce Absences by Closer Management," *The National Report on Work & Family* 13, no. 22 (November 14, 2000): 205.

55. Hochschild, *The Time Bind,* 169–70.

56. Nelson and Smith, *Working Hard and Making Do,* 72.

57. Betty Holcomb, "Friendly for Whose Family?" *MS* (April/May 2000): 40–45. Almost 80 percent of workers whose family income is in the lowest 25 percent quartile cannot be absent because of personal illness or the need to care for a sick child. Almost 60 percent cannot take vacation leave or change their working hours. Almost 40 percent cannot freely take a break. Cited in "On the Job: Freedom by Income," *New York Times,* 13 May 2001: WK 20. Data taken from Jody Heymann, *The Widening Gap* (New York: Basic Books, 2001). A study funded by the Packard Foundation found that flextime was available to 62 percent of those workers whose family income was above $71,600 but was available to only 31 percent of those with family incomes below $28,000. Tamar Lewin, "Study Says Little Has Changed in Views on Working Mothers," *New York Times,* 9 October 2001: A20.

58. Richard K. Caputo, "Race and Marital History as Correlates of Women's Access to Family-Friendly Employee Benefits," *Journal of Family and Economic Issues* 21, no. 4 (Winter 2000), 379.

59. Lisa Benenson, editor-in-chief, *Working Mother,* quoted in "Children," *New York Times Magazine,* 23 July 2000: 60.

60. Virginia E. Schein, *Working from the Margins: Voices of Mothers in Poverty* (Ithaca, N.Y.: Cornell University Press, 1995), 49.

61. Thomas E. Lengyel, ed. *Faces of Change: Personal Experiences of Welfare Reform in America* (Milwaukee, Wisc.: Alliance for Children & Families, 2001), 25.

62. Barnett and Rivers, *She Works He Works,* 60.

63. Vicky Lovell and Hedieh Rahmanou, "Paid Family and Medical Leave: Essential Support for Working Women and Men," (Washington, D.C.: Institute for Women's Policy Research, 2000), #A124.

64. Public Law 103-3, February 5, 1993, 107 STAT.9.

65. Elizabeth Olson, "U.N. Surveys Paid Leave for Mothers," *New York Times,* 16 February 1998: A5.

66. Commission on Leave, *A Workable Balance: Report to Congress on Family and Medical Leave Policies* (1996), cited in Lovell and Rahmanou, "Paid Family and Medical Leave."

67. Fried, *Taking Time,* 132.

68. Commission on Leave, Tables 5.H. and 5.R. See also R. M. Spalter-Roth and H. I. Hartmann, *Unnecessary Loses: Cost to Americans of the Lack of a Family and*

Medical Leave (Washington, D.C.: Institute for Women's Policy Research, 1990), 44.

69. Of the OECD countries, only South Korea and Switzerland have no national policy; only the United States, Australia, and New Zealand have policies providing unpaid leave, but the length of leave provided by Australia and New Zealand is a full year. Sheila B. Kamerman, "Parental Leave Policies: An Essential Ingredient in Early Childhood Education and Care Policies," *Social Policy Report* 14, no. 2 (2000): 4.

70. See Linda Kintz, *Between Jesus and the Market: The Emotions that Matter in Right-Wing America* (Durham, N.C.: Duke University Press, 1997).

71. These two seemingly disparate worlds do come together. Social conservative George Gilder praises unregulated entrepreneurialism and considers profit-making a measure of one's altruism. George Gilder, "The Soul of Silicon," *Forbes* (1 June 1998); originally a presentation given at the Vatican in May, 1991.

72. www.time.com/time/poy2001/covers/nineties. Turner was the choice in 1991; Andrew Grove of Intel in 1997; and Jeff Bezos of Amazon.com in 1999.

73. Found in Purpose #3 of Public Law 103-3.

74. Robert Heilbroner, *The Nature and Logic of Capitalism* (New York: W. W. Norton, 1985), 115–17.

75. Lengyel, ed., *Faces of Change,* 165.

76. Melvin L. Oliver and Thomas M. Shapiro, *Black Wealth/White Wealth: A New Perspective on Racial Inequality* (New York: Routledge, 1995), 96.

77. Randy Albelda and Chris Tilly, *Glass Ceilings and Bottomless Pits: Women's Work, Women's Poverty* (Boston: South End Press, 1997), 37.

78. Washington Alliance of Technology Workers, "Holiday in Amazonia," *Industry News*, 21 December 1998.

79. Presidential Press Release, "President Clinton: Raising the Minimum Wage, An Overdue Pay Raise for America's Working Families," 1/8/01; available from wo-hunger-hu-admin@pousa.org.

80. Pamela Loprest, "How Families That Left Welfare Are Doing: A National Picture" (Washington, D.C.: Urban Institute, 1999), 3. Michigan Works! Agencies reported an average wage in late 1999 of $6.65 per hour for current and former welfare recipients who are working. "The State of Working Michigan," a Michigan Budget and Tax Policy Project of the Michigan League for Human Services, Lansing, Mich., 31 August 2000.

81. Steven Greenhouse, "New York Advance in Employment Led by Low-Wage Jobs," *New York Times*, 10 January 2000: 1.56. In New York, since 1993, the number of jobs paying less than $25,000 has grown four times faster than those paying $25,000 to $75,000, and twice as fast as those paying over $75,000. Between 1989 and 1999 the median wage of low-wage workers dropped by two percent (in real dollars).

82. Louis Uchitelle, "Living In Denial, Comfortably, In a Big Home," *New York Times*, 10 June 2001: BU4.

83. Felicia Schwartz, "Management Women and the New Facts of Life," *Harvard Business Review* (Jan.-Feb., 1989): 65–76. Schwartz did not use the term "mommy track."

84. Fried, *Taking Time*, 43.

85. Cynthia Fuchs Epstein, Carroll Seron, Bonnie Oglensky, and Robert Sauté, *The Part-Time Paradox: Time Norms, Professional Life, Family and Gender* (New York: Routledge, 1999), 134–36.

86. Shannon Garrett, "Part-Time Opportunities for Professionals and Managers," (Washington, D.C.: Institute for Women's Policy Research, 1998), #A122.

87. Epstein et al., *Part-Time Paradox*, 5.

88. Ibid., 56.

89. Garrett, "Part-Time Opportunities," 5.

90. Rochelle Sharpe, "Family Friendly Firms Don't Always Promote Females," *Wall Street Journal* , 4 January 1995: B-1. See also Jeanne M. Brett, "Family, Sex, and Career Advancement," in *Integrating Work and Family: Challenges and Choices for a Changing World*, ed. Saroj Parasuraman and Jeffrey Greenhaus (Westport, Conn.: Praeger, 1999), 145–51.

91. Virginia Valian, *Why So Slow? The Advancement of Women* (Cambridge, Mass.: MIT Press, 1998), chap. 7.

92. Teresa Amott and Julie Matthaei, *Race, Gender, and Work: A Multi-Cultural Economic History of Women in the United States*, rev. ed. (Boston: South End Press, 1996), 26. In 1990, 60 percent of European American women workers, 70 percent of African American women workers, and 76 percent of Chicana workers work in the secondary labor market (345). See also Janet C. Gornick and Jerry A. Jacobs, "A Cross-National Analysis of the Wages of Part-Time Workers: Evidence from the United States, The United Kingdom, Canada, and Australia," *Work, Employment, and Society* 10, no. 1 (March 1996): 1–27.

93. Arne Kaellberg et al., "Nonstandard Work, Substandard Jobs: Flexible Work Arrangements in the U.S." (Washington, D.C.: Economic Policy Institute Study, 1997). Internet: www.epinet.org/studies/nonstandardes.html.

94. Gornick and Jacobs, "A Cross-National Analysis," 3. Chris Tilly, *Short Hours, Short Shrift: Causes and Consequences of Part-Time Work* (Washington, D.C.: Economic Policy Institute, 1990), 20. Tilly points out that involuntary full-time workers are largely workers in skilled jobs whose employers fear that it is too costly to allow them to work part-time (and continue providing benefits and high wages to keep them). He reports that about one-fourth of part-time workers do not choose voluntarily to work part-time. See also Richard J. Boden, Jr., "Flexible Working Hours, Family Responsibilities, and Female Self-Employment: Gender Differences in Self-Employment Selection, *American Journal of Economics and Sociology* 58, no. 1 (January 1999): 71–83.

95. Epstein et al., *Part-Time Paradox*, 172 n. 85, from Bureau of Labor Statistics, *Employment and Earnings*, 1997.

96. Andolsen, *The New Job Contract*, 44–45.

97. Ibid.

98. Diana M. Pearce, "The Self-Sufficiency Standard: A New Tool for Evaluating Anti-Poverty Policy," *Poverty & Race* 10, no. 2 (March/April 2001): 3–7.

99. Nina Bernstein, "In New York, Family Costs Rise Far Above Poverty Line," *New York Times*, 13 September 2000: A27.

100. Schein, *Working from the Margins*, 45.

101. Lengyel, ed., *Faces of Change*, 217.

102. Katie Hafner, "Working at Home Today?" *New York Times*, 2 November 2000: D1, D8.

103. Mark Tausig and Rudy Fenwick, "Unbinding Time: Alternate Work Schedules and Work-Life Balance," *Journal of Family and Economic Issues* 22, no.2 (Summer 2001): 101–19.

104. Hafner, "Working at Home Today."

105. Fraser, *White-Collar Sweatshop*, 25.

106. Ibid., 75.

107. "Casio Phone-Mate Report: Managing Messages in a Wired World," report of research conducted by Yankelovich Partners, March, 1998, cited in Fraser, *White-Collar Sweatshop*, 78.

108. Lengyel, ed., *Faces of Change*, 46.

109. Lottee Bailyn, *Breaking the Mold: Women, Men, and Time in the New Corporate World* (New York: Free Press, 1993), x–xi.

110. Only about 3 percent of the work force work at home, slightly more women than men. Over 90 percent are white. More than half work thirty-five or more hours per week and earn less than $14,999 per year. U.S. Census Bureau, Population Division, Journey-to-Work and Migration Statistics Branch; available at www.census.gov/population/www/socdemo/workathome/wkhtab1.html (last revised 2 November 2000). See also Barbara R. Rowe, Kathryn Stafford, Alma J. Owen, "Who's Working at Home: The Types of Families Engaged in Home-based Work," *Journal of Family and Economic Issues* 13, no. 2 (Summer 1992): 159–72. The data that follows is taken from a 1988 study in a nine-state area, "At-Home Income Generation: Impact on Management, Productivity, and Stability in Rural/Urban Families," described in R. K. Z. Heck, A. J. Owen and B. R. Rowe, *Home-based Employment and Family Life* (Westport, Conn.: Auburn House, 1995).

111. Charles Hennon, Suzanne Loker, and Rosemary Walker, "Home-based Employment: Considering Issues of Gender," in *Gender and Home-based Employment*, ed. Charles Hennon, Suzanne Loker, and Rosemary Walker (Westport, Conn.: Auburn House, 2000), 6–10.

112. Barbara Paleczny, *Clothed in Integrity: Weaving Just Cultural Relations and the Garment Industry* (Waterloo, Ontario: Wilfrid Laurier University Press for Canadian Corporation for Studies in Religion, 2000), 4.

113. Hennon and Loker, "Gender and Home-based Employment in a Global Economy," in *Gender and Home-based Employment*, ed. Hennon et al., 21.

114. Hilary Silver, "The Demand for Homework: Evidence from the U.S. Census," in *Homework: Historical and Contemporary Perspectives on Paid Labor at Home*, ed. Eileen Boris and Cynthia Daniels (Urbana, Ill.: University of Illinois Press, 1989), 116.

115. Paleczny, *Clothed in Integrity*, xviii.

116. Jamie Faricellia Dangler, "Electronics Subassemblers in Central New York: Nontraditional Homeworkers in a Nontraditional Homework Industry," in *Homework*, ed. Boris and Daniels, 155.

117. Virginia du Rivage and David Jacobs, "Home-based Work: Labor's Choices," in *Homework*, ed. Boris and Daniels, 261. In the same volume, see Cynthia Daniels, "Between Home and Factory: Homeworkers and the State," for a description of immigrant women and children as homeworkers in the late 1800s. Paleczny, *Clothed in Integrity*, 7.

118. Paleczny, *Clothed in Integrity*, 7.

119. Ibid., 4–5.

120. Ibid. This tiered organization of work also describes other industries, such as the automotive.

5

Hitting Home

What look like female values are regulations of society at large: to protect, conserve, love and rescue life. It is because these are demanded as actions or attitudes from individual women, and not from a social structure, that women are oppressed.[1]

*H*OW A SOCIETY ORGANIZES the necessary work of social reproduction (access to basic needs, the care of dependent persons, nurturance, and socialization) in relationship to the work of material production is a matter of social justice. The social science data just reviewed attest to the unjust pattern that this relationship takes in the United States. These data document how unjust structures of gender power, deepened by racism and economic exploitation, deny all women social equality. They ensnare women in exploitative relations with one another as each struggles to sustain her own family's well-being. Every family is hit by forces that diminish and deprecate family work and relations of mutuality. Some are deprived of the basic minimums of livelihood. Others maintain livelihood at the cost of just relations.

At the beginning of a new century, neoliberal economic policies and values have drawn most women into an economy of low-wage work while, at the same time, shrinking the sense of a social responsibility for the well-being of families and the quality of neighborhoods they inhabit. Shrill proclamations of support for "family values" mask a harsh and miserly public response to the needs of families. Having been taught to fear government, Americans are now being taught a Social Darwinism by the daily practices of business. It erodes our social consciousness and numbs our social empathy. By setting free the full power of the political economy to pursue capital accumulation at the expense of families and communities, this organization of human work blocks significant social transformation toward more egalitarian patterns not only for women but for families, the human community and, ultimately, for the web of earthlife itself.

Mainstream Christian ethics has long insisted, with little success, that the economy be subservient to ethical criteria that protect human dignity and livelihood. However, in the absence of a conscious and intentional analysis of socially constructed differences among humans, differences of race, gender, and economic location, privileged, white, masculine assumptions provide the context for defining dignity and livelihood. It is no accident that the characteristics of American life that now threaten American community and its families are the characteristics of this "economic man."[2] Nancy Folbre describes the theoretical schizophrenia of capitalism's economic man:

> . . . a rational decision-maker who weighs costs and benefits. . . . All his decisions are motivated by the desire to maximize his own utility—to make himself happy. In the competitive marketplace, where he constantly buys and sells, he is entirely selfish, doesn't care at all about other people's utility. In the home, however, he is entirely altruistic, loves his wife and children as much as his very self.[3]

Whatever his personal needs for intimacy, he is fundamentally "the separative self," the autonomous self, unaffected by social influences and laudably lacking "sufficient emotional connection . . . to make empathy possible."[4] In this man's world, women's and families' well-being is assumed to be a derivative of his behavior: his employment, his benefits, his wages, but also his production decisions, his financing priorities, and his distributive choices. An individual woman's and family's lack of well-being is typically associated with her unnatural attempt to sustain livelihood without dependence on a man.

With a thick description of material reality—a description of women's work to sustain their families despite their unequal social vulnerabilities—the realities of women's differing lives appear, lives never neatly divided into those abstract compartments of culture, economy, and government. Women's lives are an integrated whole. In their workplaces, neighborhoods, homes and intimate relations, the values of the economy, the state, and cultural institutions converge in embodied practices. Sometimes cooperating, sometimes conflicting, these embodied values are always interwoven into the fabric of one life lived in relationship with seen and unseen others. Together, whether conforming or resisting, these are lives lived within a larger, unifying social formation. Despite the dominant myth of separate spaces, women and their families cannot shut out by the hour, by the day, by gender, or by space the impact of the demands created by market-oriented activities from the activities of family-sustaining work. The action of the political economy shapes options for women and other family members simply because it provides or denies adequate access to material well-being. More profoundly, as a social formation, the political economy sets parameters within which is formed society's sense of moral possibilities and, consequently, socially prescribed ideals of personal and social responsibilities. As Iris Young reminds us, oppression in a liberal democratic society does not take the form of overt coercion, but is "embedded in unquestioned norms, habits, and symbols, in the assumptions underlying institutional rules and the collective consequences of following those rules."[5]

The original notion of classical liberalism—that the morality taught in family and community life would place moral limits on economic behavior—was doomed to fail. It has failed. It failed, in part, because it assumed that a political economy shaped by a socially constructed expression of elite, white masculinity would be adequate to the material and relational needs of human community. It failed because, by sanctifying the primacy of competitive, self-interested economic activities, it exempted them from the responsibility to intentionally consider the issues and moralities needed to sustain families and communities. It failed by separating from the economy any responsibility for its use of and impact on the natural or social environment. It failed because it did not and does not face up to the role that racism, sexism, and class exploitation play in shaping this economy's material success. It fails to acknowledge the actual connections between the deprivation of low-wage workers and the lifestyle of others. The undeniable results of unprecedented economic growth, quantitatively and qualitatively, are celebrated with an innocent willingness to "maximize opportunities at the top of the distribution, even if that means having significant gaps between the top and the bottom of the distribution."[6] Produced by the unquestioned norms, habits, symbols, and rules that have advantaged elite white men, this structure provides a self-affirming but cruel response to the lack of women's equality and families' well-being. By digging through the details it is revealed as a structure of disadvantage and oppression for all women and, more especially, for women and men of color and their families.

I have argued for a deep investigation of the differing realities of women's lives. However, the social sciences, including economics data, are, like all knowledge, situated. What they reveal is never disconnected from the experiences, gender, social class, and so forth, of their producers. Researchers bring to their work their often unspoken values and commitments. As "default" assumptions, values and commitments influence the type of questions that arise and seem worthy of study as well as the analyses developed to explore chosen issues. Default assumptions fill in the ordinary world and set the context in which the story that is told or the theory that is advanced may proceed.[7] One task of an ethicist is to weigh the appropriateness of the set of values and commitments embedded behind the data and its presentation that makes the story coherent.

Both the data that I chose to present, as well as the logic of my presentation, have been shaped by my commitment to women's economic rights as the necessary basis for women achieving and fully exercising social equality. My presentation has also been strongly influenced by another value-shaped observation: that, with the exception of some feminist ethicists, most economic ethics is written with little or no specific attention to the work experiences of women. One consequence of this gap in Christian economic ethics is that recent attention to family issues in Christian ethics has not been informed by a close analysis of women's work. Without that analysis, the danger arises that what one may advocate in one arena, the workplace, for example, may create unintentional harm in another, the family, or vice versa.

Family Values in Right-Wing Christianity

For example, in response to the ongoing erosion of protections for family life, right-wing Christian conservatives advocate a return to separate gendered tasks and places.[8] For them, the feminist vision of social equality represents the heart of moral decline: women rejecting God-given gender roles and men losing their God-given masculine identities as family providers. The result is gender and social chaos. Women have to assume the double work shift of both caring for homes and working for wages.

Single mothers turn to government programs to secure the food, shelter, and child support that is the God-given responsibility of husbands. Children grow up confused, unattended, in unstable homes, and in an increasingly violent society. From this perspective, feminism is destroying families, and the break-up of the family undermines society. This lament is shared by political conservatives who agree that feminism is highly dangerous. It is dangerous because it threatens the capitalist political economy. According to Irving Kristol,

> If you de-legitimize this bourgeois society, the market economy—almost incidentally, as it were—is also de-legitimized. It is for this reason that radical feminism today is a far more potent enemy of capitalism than radical trade unionism.[9]

They are correct. Right-wing Christianity and political conservatism recognize correctly that women's unpaid family work sustains the masculine identity not only of individual men but of the economic system itself. The economic vulnerability of women and children forces all men to submit themselves to the discipline of the "free" labor market. In return, all men receive socially sanctioned privileges over women and children, and, if economically successful, some men gain power over other men. The irony of the right-wing Christian position is that as neoliberal capitalism undermines the conservative family goal by reducing most men's earning capacities and drawing mothers into low-wage work, the conservative focus on the family provides its camouflage. Ultimately, in the face of neoliberalism, to sustain its gender dichotomy, right-wing Christianity will need to adopt a class analysis.

Family Values in Free Market Christianity

In the broader mainstream of Christian ethics, however, support for blatant gender inequality based on distinct, presumably complementary, social roles is not typically voiced. Whether it is actually overcome, as ethicists consider the economy and the family, is a more complex question. Michael Novak, for example, shares with the Christian Right full confidence in the basic coherence of capitalist and Christian values. This confidence underlies his conviction that cultures, including family forms, must be structured to produce the type of citizen whose virtues lead to success in free-market capitalism. For Novak, the isolated, nuclear family form is key. Its emphasis on individuals, rather than an extended family network, prepares members for the discipline of capitalism. In the nuclear family, and apparently only in that type of family, one learns a sense of self-worth based on earned accomplishment, self-discipline, the desire to better oneself, and the ability to delay gratification.[10] According to Novak, traditional families, rural families, and ethnic families, with their allegiances to extended kinship ties, cannot make a successful transition to the urban, pluralistic milieu and its work-oriented discipline of time and relationships. Thus, democratic capitalism requires a "new communitarian individual": a worker who is highly mobile, uprooted often, detached, solitary, making temporary partnerships according to the needs of the task, and moving on. Novak concludes that "Intimate proximity is not essential to community."[11] However, Novak did not mention women or gender issues in his massive 459-page work, *The Spirit of Democratic Capitalism.*

A decade later Novak became gender inclusive: "the personal economic initiative is a fundamental human right [and] to exercise that right is to fulfill the image of God inherent in every man and woman."[12] Thus, creating wealth through the free market is the fulfillment of Christian men *and women's* vocation. If we are to take Novak's gender inclusivity seriously, then, women, too, may pursue "herculean economic activities" as an expression of the *imago dei.*[13] She, too, will be a worker who is highly mobile, making temporary partnerships according to the needs of the task, solitary, and detached. She, too, will find intimate proximity inessential to community. Perhaps to be successful, then, women will be like those highly committed workers described by Carnoy "who never sleep, never consume, never have children, and never spend time socializing outside of work."[14] Women will, as some of the early gnostics recommended, become like men. Or, using Novak's analogy, women will discipline their bodies and feelings to become monk-like workers, moving and responding obediently to the needs of capital.[15]

In 1982 the "default" assumptions that sustained Novak's description of the communitarian individual worker reflected the context of an affluent male, professional and skilled. Novak did not have in mind the majority of male workers who do not move easily and successfully from one good job to a better one. He did not have women workers, who are also wives and mothers, in mind. Behind the communitarian individual, and out of his sight, was the work of families nurtured by an invisible, unpaid, dependent wife/mother. By adding women to his description of the successful worker in democratic capitalism, the cost sustained by families and communities is uncovered. Who cares for families when all minds are formed with the entrepreneurial values that turn women's, as well as men's, time into money and teach women, as well as men, to measure relationships by their use value? Faced with this dilemma, free-market proponents typically argue (and advocate) that women "choose" to prioritize caregiving responsibilities. Since the inhospitable climate of the neoliberal political economy makes any other "choice" virtually impossible, women's unequal vulnerability continues.

Family Values in Liberal Christianity

Novak exemplifies a problem that also plagues Christian ethicists more liberal than he. Neither gender justice nor family well-being can be achieved by simply stirring women into a political economy that has, since its formation, intentionally excluded "good" women and all of what was stereotypically feminine. Today, only in the abstract can it be said that women's access to wage work is evidence of gender equality. Only by accepting words for actions can one say that corporations have shown themselves to be friendly to families and nanny-ish. The problem is that without close consideration of economic contexts, even liberal Christian approaches to the well-being of families may harm women and their families unintentionally.

One example of a recent liberal ideal for Christian families is the proposed "new egalitarian family." With a specific rejection of unequal power relations between wives and husbands, Don Browning and his co-authors propose that Christian churches adopt as a family ideal "*the committed, intact, equal-regard, public-private family.*"[16] Parents in a committed, lifelong relationship should raise their biological children together while sharing in a roughly equal way the work of family, employment, and civic activities. Essentially, Browning has adopted the 1960s family ideal of Betty Friedan and the National Organization for Women as the postmodern Christian ideal. However, a key linchpin of this ideal is that each parent would work what is currently considered a part-time job—about thirty hours a week.[17] Caring for one's own children would then become possible as parents schedule themselves for differing work shifts.

In addition to the stress that working different shifts places on working-class spouses, several questionable economic assumptions lie behind this proposal. One is that the economy can create, and can be persuaded to create, part-time jobs that pay the same rate as full-time jobs and provide the same benefits. Presuming for a moment that this is possible, one question that arises is how many full-time, dual-earner families can afford to cut their income by 20 percent or more as they reduce employed hours from eighty (two full-time jobs) to sixty (two part-time jobs) per week? Currently, about three-fourths of all mothers work an average of thirty hours per week. [18] How do these families survive if husbands reduce their hours also? As the economic data have shown, most U.S. families cannot afford to reduce their working hours, even at full-time hourly wages and benefits, and still sustain a mid-level standard of living.

Moreover, a close reading of economic practices revealed that good part-time jobs exist only for a very few privileged professionals, and at a professional cost to women who primarily choose them. In fact, the entire thrust of the economy today goes in the opposite direction of this proposal. The neoliberal economy uses part-time work and easily disposable workers as tools for increased efficiency while working full-time workers longer hours at lower wages. Economic efficiency shapes the time of business where time is money. On the contrary, shorter hours for employees decreases the pool of unemployed workers, giving more power to those employed and raising the cost of hiring new workers as well as reimbursing current employees. [19] There is no evidence that businesses would acquiesce in such cost-raising restrictions. Nor is there any evidence of a political will to rein in economic forces. On the contrary, neoliberalism is a celebration of the reign of economic rationality. Without fundamental changes in the political economy, this proposal is simply unrealistic.

Is there harm in proposing an ideal? History has shown that there is. In the actual economic context of women and men, a context of increasing economic stress even for two-earner families, a family ideal that only a few, economically elite families can consider functions to sustain an oppressive status quo. Again, families and the presumably "private" choices they make become the focus of ethical concern—not the political economy that is abandoning them. When families are privatized and made the target for reform, without economic analysis, family distress and survival strategies tend to be explained in universalizing, psychological terms. For example, Browning and his co-authors turn to "expressive individualism" to explain the origins of the family crisis. Yet, as we have seen, this charge may be applicable only to a particular group—in this case a racially and economically privileged group. [20] However, by universalizing one privileged group's experiences, the material differences that exist among families because of racism and lack of adequate economic resources are dismissed as secondary factors, at best. [21] The ideal of the privileged few becomes a social ideology. Families working long hours are given a reason to blame themselves for family problems, rather than analyzing the profit-focused demands of the economy. "Good" families, those with enough education, skills, and affluence to achieve the ideal, are provided a false, self-congratulatory explanation for their own success and a self-legitimating explanation for the failure of others. Family ideals based on privileged social locations sustain the cruel innocence of the privileged and the harmful economic arrangements that create "others."

Perhaps it could be argued that such an ideal is still valid as a social *goal* for which to strive. This suggestion highlights another troubling economic presumption behind the proposal. That couples should work in market-oriented activities *no longer* than sixty hours a week implies that some families can and should choose to reduce their income-producing hours without economic jeopardy. As we have seen, some higher-earning families could make this choice. However, what remains unclear is whether a sixty-hour workweek is now assumed to be the *norm* for maintaining a middle-income family's standard of living. This appears to be the case since these authors argue that single mothers receiving welfare assistance should also be employed for thirty hours a week in order to equal the work effort expected of a married mother.[22]

As a *norm*, not merely a choice, this proposal unintentionally replaces for most families the long sought goal of a forty-hour, family-sustaining workweek. Even though sixty hours are divided between two adults, this should not mask the major concession to the economy that this proposal makes in terms of the share of family time that will be absorbed by market-oriented work. It returns families to the ten-hour days and six-day workweek of the nineteenth century. The impact of a norm of a sixty-hour family workweek on single mother families who do not receive public assistance would be disastrous. Today, the '50s ideal of a forty-hour, family-sustaining workweek seems like another radical, left-wing utopian idea. Recent proposals, such as the Iowa City Declaration for a thirty to thirty-two hour workweek, are simply absent from serious public discourse.[23] When a sixty-hour workweek seems like a *reduction* in time that workers spend away from the family, the devastating power with which neoliberal economic policies have shaped the common sense becomes startlingly clear.

Ultimately, liberal Christian proposals fail because they assume that gender equality and family well-being can be achieved by encouraging women to enter the same work world as men. They fail because they do not realize the antifeminine, that is, anti-caring, character of this economy. And they fail because they do not admit the connections: that the success of some women, mostly white women, in balancing employment and family life depends on the hard struggle of other women, mostly women of color, to simply sustain their families.

In order to bring this structure of oppression to an end, to address this injustice in ways that have the potential to break out of the imposed limits of capitalist moral imagination, a feminist liberative Christian economic ethics begins from new (to this political economy) moral principles.

The Full Equality of Women

The most obvious is the affirmation of the self-worth of women as full participatory citizens and moral agents. Just as obvious, this claim is not new. Women have been making the claim of essential human equality for centuries, perhaps millennia. Yet the claim remains new because it is an expression of that which is still denied. A Christian feminist economic ethics requires a political economy shaped by and accountable to *women's* dignity and livelihood, whether or not women choose to participate in heterosexual relationships, whether or not they marry, whether or not they bear children. However, in this political economy where autonomy and isolated individualism are assumed to be the human norm, being a woman, being an actual or potential mother or caregiver, increases economic vulnerability. In this political economy where the *lack* of caregiving responsibilities and dependency is assumed to be the human norm, being an actual or potential mother or caregiver is a liability. The equality of women requires a political economy in which being an actual or potential mother, being in need of care, and being responsible for the care of others, *are* the human norm.

Resistance to current patterns of injustice and the creation of more gender equal and community-supporting practices can begin with many small steps. Many are compatible with liberal agendas. The difference is in the final goal, an inclusive economic democracy, and the length of the struggle. Specific suggestions of ways to move the political economy into women- and caregiver-friendly practices abound. Most obvious is the need to make women's wage work pay through policies of comparable worth and affirmative action that undo embedded white, male privileges.

But even if the gender and racial disparities in wages were eliminated, women and men, mothers and fathers, cannot afford to choose equal parenting and caregiving as long as workplace and public policies favor those who do no dependent-care work—men or women. A public commitment to women's equality and the actual implementation of shared parenting and caregiving depends on the elimination of all forms of discrimination against caregivers and the dismantling of all forms of advantage for those who are not caregivers. Some relatively modest suggestions attempt to provide economic security for those men or women who *voluntarily* choose to do the traditionally unpaid work of family caregiving. For example, Okin suggests that both partners in a marriage have equal legal entitlement to all earnings entering the household.[24] Folbre adds that without changing the basic structure of Social Security each partner could be given credit for half of the total income entering the family as the basis for their claim to old-age insurance.[25] She and many others have called for some form of family allowance: that is, public compensation for the value of family labor regardless of income level or biological relationship, or family form. Family allowances, as well as tax deductions, help to defray the cost of dependent care and serve, again, as a public recognition of the value to society of this labor.[26] Mary Hobgood points out that a social commitment to women's equality necessitates providing women, particularly low-income women, with alternatives to abusive partners, exploitative work, and punitive government assistance.[27] Many European countries already provide universal healthcare, childcare, and retirement benefits, as well as generous (by U.S. standards) paid parental and family leave, paid vacation time and unemployment policies.[28] Alternative models to U.S. neoliberalism do exist at modest costs. It has been estimated that if the costs of maternity, paternity, and parental benefits were added together, the total would amount to less than 1 percent of the Gross Domestic Product of any OECD country, with the exceptions of Finland and Sweden.[29] It is a question of values, not costs.

Moreover, economic practices must be disciplined to harmonize with family and community activities. The length of the average workday must be reduced and harmonized with school schedules. Minimum wages for no more than a forty-hour workweek (and preferably less) should place a family of three at a threshold of self-sufficiency adjusted to the specific locale. The cost to companies of workers working overtime should be severe, including taxes that would help support community-provided dependent-care services. In other words, the practice of business must not only produce a product or service, but a citizenry that is expected, encouraged, and enabled to attend to the needs and activities of familial, cultural, and democratic institutions.

Socializing the "Feminine"

A second principle of a Christian feminist liberative economic ethic is the full incorporation into the political economy of the *social* value of the stereotypical virtues of the feminine. That is, who we are as moral agents-in-relationships-of-care-and-trust should not (cannot, does not) metamorphose in the commute to and from the workplace. Therefore, the character of productive work must be transformed to be congruent with and complementary to the values and practices traditionally called "feminine." The morality needed to sustain family and community life must also shape the nature and practices of the economy.

This is part of a necessary conversion from what Rasmussen calls "economic messianism": that is, trust in the process of rational economic development to lead to human fulfillment without much need for thinking ethically.[30] Incorporating the value of caregiving, caregivers, and those who need care into the economy is part of the conversion to a sufficient, sustainable earth community for all. The external costs of downsizing and plant closings, as well as the depletion of natural resources and polluting of the environment, have to be internalized. The social harms of economic practices that in today's economic system reflect the self-interest of some have to be accounted for—and compensated for—as a recognition of the social mortgage with which all private property is held. [31] The assumption that families naturally produce a new generation of workers—and only err by producing too many or too few—can be challenged by the economic recognition that children are a social good requiring a response of social support. The recognition that all individuals "receive loans from their family, from other people, and from the global environment that allow them to develop their human and social capital" could lead to a broader sense of social responsibilities.[32] Those who benefit from the work of dependent care—businesses needing employees, the elderly needing the labor of the younger generation, all of us—should help to pay for it. This is not a new economic principle. Folbre explains in the language of classical economics:

> . . . the costs of social reproduction must be paid. . . . Like the costs of a healthy environment, they are largely external to the market economy. But these externalities constrain its long-run possibilities of success. One might suggest, following the standard precepts of neoclassical theory, that the private and social rates of return to childbearing should be brought into balance—those who receive the benefits should also pay the costs.[33]

What seems new is the path required to reach this goal: economic democracy. However, the goal of economic democracy is not new even to the United States. "Industrial democracy" was a term used by Woodrow Wilson and Franklin D. Roosevelt as part of their common argument that the success of a political democracy required a more egalitarian economy as determined by workers' needs and interests. It was a term used by labor priests and the theologians of the social gospel at the turn of the last century: Walter Rauschenbusch and John Ryan, for example.[34] Their arguments are as pertinent today as then. The determination of who should bear which social burdens and how benefits should be shared must ultimately be made through inclusive, democratic processes that are weighted toward the most vulnerable. Then economics will be defined as economist Julie Nelson suggests: a discipline "centrally concerned with the study of how humans, in interaction with each other and the environment, provide for their own survival and health," with the recognition that "survival" requires the well-being of children and families and "health" requires purposeful work and the enjoyment of life.[35]

Valuing Families

A third principle of a Christian feminist liberative economic ethic is the recognition that the family—in its diverse forms—is an important site in the struggle for gender, racial, and economic justice.[36] Much of feminist analysis of the family has identified the role of families in the reproduction of social injustice. However, feminist analyses also reveal the importance of family forms and intrafamily relations in the work of challenging that injustice. In fact, justice within families is critical to the creation of social justice, and vice versa. Over twenty years ago psychologist Nancy Chodorow ascribed the reproduction of modern society's gender inequality to the construction of children's gendered identities within the traditional, gender-dichotomized, nuclear family.[37] In societies that structure unequal gender roles, she argued, the exclusive nurturing of boys and girls by mothers produces gendered personalities consistent with those social roles: women's domesticity and men's dominance. At the same time, unjust social structures limit family options such that gendered identities are reproduced to re-affirm existing social structures.

Ten years later, Susan Moller Okin, a political scientist, made a strong feminist case for the centrality of the family as a formative environment in which children learn the meaning of justice.[38] As children experience their first powerful example of adult interaction, of the way roles and responsibilities are divided and decisions are made among adults, and as they experience parental love and learn to reciprocate it, Okin argued, children embody a meaning of justice and love that they will carry into social relations. Within the so-called traditional nuclear family with its gender dichotomy, children have learned to accept a sense of justice that accommodates women's unequal economic vulnerability. More broadly, children learn that justice is satisfied despite the socially constructed inequality embedded in gendered, racial, and class relations. However, in the everyday practices of families, children could also learn the practices and explanations with which to challenge social injustice. Okin is quick to point out that families cannot do this without the support of both social and economic policies. With Chodorow she concludes that the achievement of social justice for women and the practice of justice within the family are interlocked.

The time, the practices, and the living example of resistance to unjust social values require what Larry Rasmussen calls "manifold engagement": practicing skills such as hospitality, learning the discipline of being one member of a community, enlarging one's sensibilities to include the needs of others, interacting with others as humans of unique value, learning and practicing justice-oriented traditions.[39] Rasmussen describes the activities that produce character—but not just any character. These are the activities that produce characters capable of sustaining just relationships, and practicing the virtues that knit together persons in inclusive, egalitarian communities. These are the practices that orient people toward a common good.

Womanist ethicists describe the time mothers spend in mothering and other-mothering as time spent in teaching skills of both survival and resistance in a society that never intended the survival of these mothers' children. The very values disparaged by Michael Novak as "ethnic" or "traditional" are described by Patricia Hill Collins as those "traditional cultural values—[that] can help people cope with and resist oppression."[40] The nuclear-family form and values often praised by some mainline Christian ethicists are identified by Collins as rooted in white, upper-income, patriarchal privileges. In marginalized communities today, as in the nineteenth century, family values are those that make survival possible for families who lack race and income privilege; who are not "ideal." They involve, as Cheryl Townsend Gilkes writes, "Reaching out . . . to single mothers, orphans, widows, and widowers . . . to come as they were."[41] In the margins, a home is a place where all the dignity that the world denies is given. bell hooks writes:

> *We could not learn to love or respect ourselves in the culture of white supremacy, on the outside; it was there on the inside, in that "homeplace," most often created and kept by black women, that we had the opportunity to grow and develop, to nurture our spirits.*[42]

Understanding families as both schools of injustice but, potentially, bearers of critical, transformative values is consistent with the strong rejection found in the New Testament of the first-century familial, social structures in Palestine. The Gospels of Matthew and Mark, especially, depict Jesus' rejection of his culture's established family forms and his redefinition of "family" for those who follow him. As Lisa Cahill and Rosemary Ruether point out, Greco-Roman and Jewish family traditions shaped families for the purposes of maintaining and strengthening privileged social relationships—to the disadvantage and disempowerment of women, slaves, children, and the poor.[43] Cahill points out that it was through the social control these families exercised that the interests of both religious and political elites were sustained. She writes: "The family in the ancient world—as in many ways today—is the nexus of relationships of social inequalities maintained by structures of precedence and subjugation."[44] Consequently, the Jesus movement developed what Rosemary Ruether calls an "antifamily" tradition as it redefined the new family calling for disciples of Jesus. Ruether writes:

> . . . as a gathering of mostly marginal men and women out of their families and occupations into a countercultural community. This community is seen as a new eschatological family that negates the natural family. No one is worthy to be a disciple who prefers his family to Jesus. . . .[45]

Christians must again recognize that the privileged Western form of the family created with the rise of capitalism has been, and is, based on unjust social arrangements. Today, global neoliberal economic pressures are destroying traditional gender identities and family forms for poor- and middle-income families around the world. But they are not being replaced with forms of greater gender equality or family well-being. Families of all sorts struggle to survive forces that brutally exceed their adaptive powers. In the United States an economy urges workers to see themselves as self-interested individuals serving "Me, Inc." and calls it "freedom." A government celebrates the reduction of virtually every kind of public support for families, contemplates requiring poor single mothers to work forty hours a week without childcare support, and advocates marriage rather than just wages as a solution to poverty. The popular discourse of family values has simply assumed that Christian values are synonymous with the neoliberal language of economic growth, individualism, and the nuclear family.[46] As both Ruether and Cahill point out, Christian history has been characterized too often by the ability of Christians to domesticate the radically inclusive, egalitarian, prophetic tradition of the early Christian movement. We are forewarned, then, that in an unjust society divided by racial, class, and gender inequalities, any socially constructed ideal form of the family is likely to be based on privileges of race, gender, and class. Today, through the examination of women's work, the nature and logic of capitalism itself is shown to undermine the radical Christian values of women's equality, the well-being of families, and the protection of earthlife. The ideals of the privileged should never be mistaken as Christian ideals.

Confronted with such a momentous challenge, a Christian feminist liberative ethic attests to both a faith in and an expectation of ongoing social re-creation. In Christian terms this occurs when women and men strive to embody more fully the meaning of divinity which they equally image by working to embed its inclusive and egalitarian values in social institutions. "[R]edemptive humanity," writes Rosemary Radford Ruether, "goes ahead of us, calling us to yet incompleted dimensions of human liberation."[47] In secular terms, transformation for those who are privileged begins with the recognition that even they are being managed in ways that demean their humanity: the heartless discipline of a work ethic expanding to control every place and every moment, increased restrictions on family life and time with children, the imposition on families of social values that serve a profit-driven economic system, the growing separation of groups based on race and income accompanied by growing fears and anxieties.[48] Christian ethics supports social conversion to the family values of Jesus when it provides a social analysis that reveals our fundamental human interconnectedness, destroys the innocence of the privileged, and works to exhibit and reestablish the social power of relationship by which we can choose to co-create one another for the better. Even in the midst of this neoliberal world . . .

> It is still within the power of love, which is the good news of God, to keep us in the knowledge that none of us were born only to die, that we were meant to have the gift of life, to know the power of relation and to pass it on.[49]

NOTES

1. Grigga Haug, "Daydreams," cited in Nancy Folbre, *Who Pays for the Kids? Gender and the Structures of Constraint* (New York: Routledge, 1994), 10.

2. See Robert Bellah, Richard Madsen, William Sullivan, Ann Swidler, and Steven Tipton, *Habits of the Heart: Individualism and Commitment in American Life* (Berkeley: University of California Press, 1985).

3. Folbre, *Who Pays for the Kids?* 18.

4. Paula England, "The Separative Self: Androcentric Bias in Neoclassical Assumptions," in *Beyond Economic Man: Feminist Theory and Economics*, ed. Marianne A. Ferber and Julie A. Nelson (Chicago: University of Chicago Press, 1993), 37.

5. Iris Marion Young, *Justice and the Politics of Difference* (Princeton, N.J.: Princeton University Press, 1990), 41.

6. Sheldon Danizer, "After welfare reform and an economic boom: why is child poverty still so much higher in the U.S. than in Europe?" paper presented at the 8th International Research Seminar of the Foundation for International Studies on Social Security, Sigtuna, Sweden, June 2001. See also Sheldon Danziger and Jane Waldfogel, eds. *Securing the Future: Investing in Children from Birth to College* (New York: Russell Sage Foundation, 2000).

7. Diana Strassman and Livia Polanyi, "The Economist as Storyteller: What the Texts Reveal," in *Out of the Margin: Feminist Perspectives on Economics*, ed. Edith Kuiper and Jolande Sap (New York: Routledge, 1995); Donald McCloskey, *If You're So Smart: The Narrative of Economic Expertise* (Chicago: University of Chicago Press, 1990).

8. Beverly LaHaye, *Desires of a Woman's Heart* (Wheaton, Ill.: Tyndale, 1993); Connie Marshner, *Can Motherhood Survive? A Christian Looks at Social Parenting* (Brentwood, Tenn.: Wolgemuth and Hyatt, 1990). For feminist analyses see Linda Kintz, *Between Jesus and the Market: The Emotions that Matter in Right-Wing America* (Durham, N.C.: Duke University Press, 1997).

9. Irving Kristol, cited in Kintz, *Between Jesus and the Market*, 50–51.

10. Michael Novak, *The Spirit of Democratic Capitalism* (Lanham, Md.: Madison Books, 1982, 1991), 163, 166–70.

11. Ibid., 55, 137, 169, 142, 137.

12. Michael Novak, *This Hemisphere of Liberty: A Philosophy of the Americas* (Washington, D.C.: American Enterprise Institute, 1992), 33.

13. Novak, *The Spirit of Democratic Capitalism*, 163.

14. Martin Carnoy, *Sustaining the New Economy: Work, Family, and Community in the Information Age* (New York: Russell Sage Foundation, 2000), 142.

15. Novak, *The Spirit of Democratic Capitalism*, 101.

16. Don S. Browning, Bonnie J. Miller-McLemore, Pamela D. Couture, K. Brynolf Lyon, and Robert M. Franklin, *From Culture Wars to Common Ground:*

Religion and the American Family Debate (Louisville, Ky.: Westminster John Knox Press, 1997), 2. Italics in the original.

17. This proposal was first set forth by Jean Bethke Elshtain and David Popenoe, *Marriage in America: A Report to the Nation* (New York: Council on Families in America of the Institute for American Values, 1995).

18. Deanna Lyter, Gi-Taik Oh, and Vicky Lovell, "New Welfare Proposals Would Require Mothers Receiving Assistance to Work More than the Average American Mom; Child Care Inadequate" (Washington, D.C.: Institute for Women's Policy Research Publication, 2002), #D445; available at www.iwpr.org.

19. Juliet Schor, *The Overworked American: The Unexpected Decline of Leisure* (New York: Basic Books, 1991), 75.

20. Browning et al., *From Culture Wars to Common Ground*, 51.

21. Ibid., 21, 64–65. While mentioned briefly, neither racism nor poverty is identified as a significant factor in the crisis of families. The result is a particular sense of "family crisis," in this case a crisis of individual values, that leads to religious and social responses to reshape values and require different behavior from individuals.

22. Ibid., 327. In 2002, the George W. Bush administration proposed that single mothers be required to work forty hours per week to remain eligible for TANF.

23. Sarah Ryan, "Management by Stress: The Reorganization of Work Hits Home in the 1990's," in *American Families: A Multicultural Reader*, ed. Stephanie Coontz, Maya Parson, and Gabrielle Raley (New York: Routledge, 1999), 339. The Iowa City Declaration was the outcome of a 1995 conference entitled "Our Time Famine: A Critical Look at the Culture of Work and a Reevaluation of 'Free Time.'"

24. Susan Moller Okin, *Justice, Gender, and the Family* (Basic Books, 1989), 181.

25. Folbre, *Who Pays for the Kids?*, 209.

26. Ibid., 121–23, 258. But tax deductions only aid those who earn enough to pay taxes. I would argue that a specific family allowance is the better form of support.

27. Mary Hobgood, "Poor Women, Work, and the U.S. Catholic Bishops," *Journal of Religious Ethics* 25, no. 2 (Fall 1997): 326.

28. Swedes currently are entitled to eighteen months of paid leave with job protection that can be prorated over the first eight years of a child's life. France provides universal childcare to all toilet-trained children. Single mothers receive government payments until their children are over the age of three. Nancy Folbre, *The Invisible Heart: Economics and Family Values* (New York: New Press, 2001), 131–35.

29. Sheila B. Kamerman, "Parental Leave Policies: An Essential Ingredient in Early Childhood Education and Care Policies," *Social Policy Report* 14, n. 2 (2000): 10.

30. Larry Rasmussen, *Earth Community Earth Ethics* (Maryknoll, N.Y.: Orbis Books, 1996), 51.

31. Daniel Finn, "John Paul II and the Moral Ecology of Markets," *Theological*

Studies 59, no. 4 (1998): 671–76. Christian ethics has long taught that a social mortgage rests upon the ownership of private property. However, I am extending the use of the concept beyond the personal responsibility to provision those lacking in basic needs with one's private property to include a moral claim to participation in prior communal decisions about what is *private* and how that decision must be made in such a way as to promote gender equality. That is, there is a social mortgage on how decision-making power is distributed in a society.

32. Folbre, *Who Pays for the Kids?*, 255.

33. Ibid., 124.

34. See Gary J. Dorrien, *Reconstructing the Common Good: Theology and the Social Order* (Maryknoll, N.Y.: Orbis Books, 1990). "Labor priest" is a term describing these Roman Catholic priests who typically served poor, immigrant parishes and included labor activism as part of their pastoral care and gospel interpretation.

35. Julie A. Nelson, "The Study of Choice or the Study of Provisioning? Gender and the Definition of Economics," in *Beyond Economic Man: Feminist Theory and Economics*, ed. Ferber and Nelson, 34, 32.

36. For several concise overviews of feminists' analyses of the family, see *The American Philosophical Association Newsletter on Feminism and Philosophy* 96, no. 1 (Fall 1996): 31–45.

37. Nancy Chodorow, *The Reproduction of Mothering: Psychoanalysis and the Sociology of Gender* (Berkeley: University of California Press, 1978).

38. Okin, *Justice, Gender, and the Family*.

39. Larry Rasmussen, *Moral Fragments and Moral Community: A Proposal for Church in Society* (Minneapolis: Fortress Press, 1993), 80.

40. Patricia Hill Collins, *Black Feminist Thought: Knowledge, Consciousness, and the Politics of Empowerment* (New York: Routledge, 1990), 122.

41. Cheryl Townsend Gilkes, "The Storm and the Light: Church, Family, Work, and Social Crisis in the African-American Experience," in *Work, Family, and Religion in Contemporary Society*, ed. Nancy T. Ammerman and Wade Clark Roof (New York: Routledge, 1995), 179.

42. bell hooks, *Yearning: race, gender, and cultural politics* (Boston: South End Press, 1990), 42.

43. Lisa Sowle Cahill, *Family: A Christian Social Perspective* (Minneapolis: Fortress Press, 2000), chap. 2; Rosemary Radford Ruether, *Christianity and the Making of the Modern Family* (Boston: Beacon Press, 2000), chap.1.

44. Cahill, *Family*, 27.

45. Ruether, *Christianity*, 25. Ruether notes that the antifamily sayings of Jesus show a "shocking disregard for traditional family responsibilities; they show an expectation that following the gospel will stir the enmity of traditional family members.

46. Janet Fishburn, *Confronting the Idolatry of Family: A New Vision for the Household of God* (Nashville: Abingdon Press, 1991).

47. Rosemary Radford Ruether, *Sexism and God-Talk: Toward a Feminist Theology* (Boston: Beacon Press, 1983), 138.

48. See Mary Elizabeth Hobgood, *Dismantling Privilege: An Ethics of Accountability* (Cleveland: Pilgrim Press, 2000), for a thorough analysis of the harms sustained by the privileged.

49. Beverly Wildung Harrison, *Making the Connections: Essays in Feminist Social Ethics*, ed. Carol S. Robb (Boston: Beacon Press, 1985), 20.

Bibliography

Abramovitz, Mimi. *Under Attack, Fighting Back: Women and Welfare in the United States.* New York: Monthly Review Press, 2000.

Albelda, Randy, and Chris Tilly. *Glass Ceilings and Bottomless Pits: Women's Work, Women's Poverty.* Boston: South End Press, 1997.

————, Robert Drago, and Steven Shulman. *Uneven Playing Fields: Understanding Wage Inequality and Discrimination.* New York: McGraw-Hill, 1997.

Albrecht, Gloria. *The Character of Our Communities: Toward an Ethic of Liberation for the Church.* Nashville: Abingdon Press, 1995.

Ammerman, Nancy T., and Wade Clark Roof, eds. *Work, Family, and Religion in Contemporary Society.* New York: Routledge, 1995.

Amott, Teresa, and Julie Matthaei. *Race, Gender, and Work: A Multi-Cultural Economic History of Women in the United States.* Rev. ed. Boston: South End Press, 1996.

Andolsen, Barbara. *The New Job Contract: Economic Justice in an Age of Insecurity.* Cleveland: Pilgrim Press, 1998.

Badaracco, Claire. "Can the Church Save Women? Public Opinion, the U.N. and the Policy Gap." *America*, 14 March 1992: 215-18.

Bailyn, Lottee. *Breaking the Mold: Women, Men, and Time in the New Corporate World.* New York: Free Press, 1993.

Barnett, Rosalind, and Caryl Rivers. *She Works He Works: How Two-Income Families Are Happier, Healthier, and Better-off.* San Francisco: HarperSanFrancisco, 1996.

Benería, Lourdes, and Shelly Feldman, eds. *Unequal Burden: Economic Crises, Persistent Poverty, and Women's Work.* Boulder, Colo.: Westview Press, 1992.

Blau, Francine D., and Ronald G. Ehrenberg, eds. *Gender and Family Issues in the Workplace.* New York: Russell Sage Foundation, 1997.

Boatright, John. *Ethics and the Conduct of Business.* Englewood Cliffs, N.J.: Prentice Hall, 1993.

Boris, Eileen, and Cynthia Daniels, eds. *Homework: Historical and Contemporary Perspectives on Paid Labor at Home.* Urbana: University of Illinois Press, 1989.

Borsook, Paulina. *Cyberselfish: A Critical Romp through the Terribly Libertarian Culture of High Tech*. New York: Public Affairs, 2000.

Bose, Christine, Roslyn Feldberg, and Natalie Sokoloff, eds. *Hidden Aspects of Women's Work*. New York: Praeger, 1987.

Bounds, Elizabeth M. *Coming Together/Coming Apart: Religion, Community, and Modernity*. New York: Routledge, 1997.

————, Pamela K. Brubaker, and Mary E. Hobgood. *Welfare Policy: Feminist Critiques*. Cleveland: Pilgrim Press, 1999.

Boydston, Jeanne. *Home and Work: Housework, Wages and the Ideology of Labor in the Early Republic*. New York: Oxford University Press, 1990.

Brenner, Johanna. *Women and the Politics of Class*. New York: Monthly Review Press, 2000.

Browning, Don S., Bonnie J. Miller-McLemore, Pamela D. Couture, K. Brynolf Lyon, and Robert M. Franklin. *From Culture Wars to Common Ground: Religion and the American Family Debate*. Louisville, Ky.: Westminster John Knox Press, 1997.

Bullock. Susan. *Women and Work*. London: Zed Books, 1994.

Cahill, Lisa Sowle. *Family: A Christian Social Perspective*. Minneapolis: Fortress Press, 2000.

Carnoy, Martin. *Sustaining the New Economy: Work, Family, and Community in the Information Age*. New York: Russell Sage Foundation, 2000.

Chodorow, Nancy. *The Reproduction of Mothering: Psychoanalysis and the Sociology of Gender*. Berkeley: University of California Press, 1978.

Collins, Chuck, Betsy Leondar-Wright, and Holly Sklar. *Shifting Fortunes: The Perils of the Growing American Wealth Gap*. Boston: United for a Fair Economy, 1999.

————, and Felice Yeskel. *Economic Apartheid in America: A Primer on Economic Inequality and Insecurity*. New York: New Press, 2000.

Collins, Patricia Hill. *Black Feminist Thought: Knowledge, Consciousness, and the Politics of Empowerment*. New York: Routledge, 1990.

Coontz, Stephanie. *The Social Origins of Private Life: A History of American Families 1600-1900*. New York: Verso, 1988.

————. *The Way We Never Were: American Families and the Nostalgia Trap*. New York: Basic Books, 1992.

————, Maya Parson, and Gabrielle Raley, eds. *American Families: A Multicultural Reader*. New York: Routledge, 1999.

Cott, Nancy F. *Public Vows: A History of Marriage and the Nation*. Cambridge: Harvard University Press, 2000.

Cottle, Thomas J. *Hardest Times: The Trauma of Long Term Unemployment*. Westport, Conn.: Praeger, 2000.

Cravey, Altha J. *Women and Work in Mexico's Maquiladoras*. New York: Rowman & Littlefield, 1998.

Crittenden, Ann. *The Price of Motherhood: Why the Most Important Job in the World Is Still the Least Valued.* New York: Metropolitan Books, 2001.

Curran, Charles, and Margaret Farley, eds. *Feminist Ethics and the Catholic Moral Tradition.* New York: Paulist Press, 1996.

Danziger, Sheldon, and Jane Waldfogel, eds. *Securing the Future: Investing in Children from Birth to College.* New York: Russell Sage Foundation, 2000.

Davis, Angela. *Women, Race, and Class.* New York: Vintage, 1983.

D'Emilio, John, and Estelle B. Freedman. *Intimate Matters: A History of Sexuality in America.* New York: Harper & Row, 1988.

Dorrien, Gary J. *Reconstructing the Common Good: Theology and the Social Order.* Maryknoll, N.Y.: Orbis Books, 1990.

Ehrenreich, Barbara. *Nickel and Dimed: On (Not) Getting By in America.* New York: Metropolitan Books, 2001.

Eisenstein, Zillah. *The Radical Future of Liberal Feminism.* Boston: Northeastern University Press, 1981.

Elshtain, Jean Bethke, and David Popenoe. *Marriage in America: A Report to the Nation.* New York: Council on Families in America of the Institute for American Values, 1995.

Epstein, Cynthia Fuchs, Carroll Seron, Bonnie Oglensky, and Robert Sauté. *The Part-Time Paradox: Time Norms, Professional Life, Family and Gender.* New York: Routledge, 1999.

Ferber, Marianne A., and Julie A. Nelson, eds. *Beyond Economic Man: Feminist Theory and Economics.* Chicago: University of Chicago Press, 1993.

Finn, Daniel R. "John Paul II and the Moral Ecology of Markets." *Theological Studies* 59, no. 4 (1998): 662-79.

Fiorenza, Elisabeth Schüssler. *Jesus: Miriam's Child Sophia's Prophet: Critical Issues in Feminist Christology.* New York: Continuum, 1995.

Fishburn, Janet. *Confronting the Idolatry of Family: A New Vision for the Household of God.* Nashville: Abingdon Press, 1991.

Folbre, Nancy. *Who Pays for the Kids? Gender and the Structures of Constraint.* New York: Routledge, 1994.

———. *The Invisible Heart: Economics and Family Values.* New York: New Press, 2001.

———, Barbara Bergmann, Bina Agarwal, and Maria Floro. *Women's Work in the World Economy.* New York: New York University Press, 1992.

Foucault, Michel. *The History of Sexuality,* trans. R. Hurley. New York: Vintage, 1980.

Fraser, Jill Andresky. *White-Collar Sweatshop: The Deterioration of Work and Its Rewards in Corporate America.* New York: W. W. Norton, 2001.

Fried, Mindy. *Taking Time: Parental Leave Policy and Corporate Culture.* Philadelphia: Temple University Press, 1998.

Friedan, Betty. *The Feminine Mystique.* New York: Laurel, 1963; reprint 1983.

Galbraith, James K. *Created Unequal: The Crisis in American Pay.* New York: Free Press, 2000.

Giddings, Paula. *When and Where I Enter: The Impact of Black Women on Race and Sex in America*. New York: Bantam Books, 1984.

Goldin, Claudia. *Understanding the Gender Gap*. New York: Oxford University Press, 1990.

Gordon, Linda. *Pitied But Not Entitled: Single Mothers and the History of Welfare, 1890–1935*. New York: Free Press, 1994.

Gramsci, Antonio. *Selections from the Prison Notebooks of Antonio Gramsci*, ed. and trans. Quinton Hoare and Geoffrey Nowell Smith. New York: International Publishers, 1972.

Grelle, Bruce, and David A. Krueger. *Christianity and Capitalism: Perspectives on Religion, Liberalism and the Economy*. Chicago: Center for the Scientific Study of Religion, 1986.

Grove, Andrew S. *Only the Paranoid Survive: How to Exploit the Crisis Points That Challenge Every Company and Career*. New York: Currency, Doubleday, 1996.

Hackstaff, Karla B. *Marriage in a Culture of Divorce*. Philadelphia: Temple University Press, 1999.

Handler, Joel, and Lucie White, eds. *Hard Labor: Women and Work in the Post-Welfare Era*. Armonk, N.Y.: M. E. Sharpe, 1999.

Hareven, Tamara K. *Family Time and Industrial Time: The Relationship Between the Family and Work in a New England Industrial Community*. Cambridge: Cambridge University Press, 1982.

Harrison, Beverly Wildung. *Making the Connections: Essays in Feminist Social Ethics*. Edited by Carol S. Robb. Boston: Beacon Press, 1985.

Heck, R. K. Z., A. J. Owen, and B. R. Rowe. *Home-based Employment and Family Life*. Westport, Conn.: Auburn House, 1995.

Heilbroner, Robert L. *The Nature and Logic of Capitalism*. New York: W. W. Norton, 1985.

Hennessy, Rosemary, and Chrys Ingraham, eds. *Material Feminism: A Reader in Class, Difference, and Women's Lives*. New York: Routledge, 1997.

Hennon, Charles, Suzanne Loker, and Rosemary Walker, eds. *Gender and Home-based Employment*. Westport, Conn.: Auburn House, 2000.

Hesse-Biber, Sharlene, and Gregg Lee Carter. *Working Women in America: Split Dreams*. New York: Oxford University Press, 2000.

Heymann, Jody. *The Widening Gap*. New York: Basic Books, 2001.

Hobgood, Mary Elizabeth. "Poor Women, Work, and the U.S. Catholic Bishops." *Journal of Religious Ethics* 25, no. 2 (Fall 1997): 307-33.

———. *Dismantling Privilege: An Ethics of Accountability*. Cleveland: Pilgrim Press, 2000.

Hochschild, Arlie Russell. *The Second Shift*. New York: Avon Books, 1989.

———. *The Time Bind: When Work Becomes Home and Home Becomes Work*. New York: Metropolitan Books, 1997.

hooks, bell. *Yearning: race, gender, and cultural politics*. Boston: South End Press, 1990.

Hopps, June Gary, Elaine Pinderhughes, and Richard Shanker. *The Power to Care: Clinical Practice Effectiveness with Overwhelmed Clients.* New York: Free Press, 1995.

Hoy, D. C., ed. *Foucault: A Critical Reader.* Oxford: Basil Blackwell, 1986.

Jackson, Kenneth. *Crabgrass Frontier: The Suburbanization of the United States.* New York: Oxford University Press, 1985.

Jacobsen, Joyce P. *The Economics of Gender.* Cambridge, Mass.: Blackwell, 1994.

Jones, Jacqueline. *American Work: Four Centuries of Black and White Labor.* New York: W. W. Norton, 1998.

———. *The Dispossessed: America's Underclasses from the Civil War to the Present.* New York: Basic Books, 1992.

———. *Labor of Love, Labor of Sorrow: Black Women, Work and the Family, from Slavery to the Present.* New York: Vintage Books, 1985.

Katz, Michael B. *The Undeserving Poor: From the War on Poverty to the War on Welfare.* New York: Pantheon Books, 1989.

King, Paul G., and David O. Woodyard. *Liberating Nature: Theology and Economics in a New Order.* Cleveland: Pilgrim Press, 1999.

Kintz, Linda. *Between Jesus and the Market: The Emotions that Matter in Right-Wing America.* Durham, N.C.: Duke University Press, 1997.

Kittay, Eva Feder. *Love's Labor: Essays on Women, Equality, and Dependency.* New York: Routledge, 1999.

Kuiper, Edith, and Jolande Sap, eds. *Out of the Margin: Feminist Perspectives on Economics.* New York: Routledge, 1995.

LaHaye, Beverly. *Desires of a Woman's Heart.* Wheaton, Ill.: Tyndale, 1993.

Lengyel, Thomas E. ed. *Faces of Change: Personal Experiences of Welfare Reform in America.* Milwaukee: Alliance for Children and Families, 2001.

Levine, James A., and Todd L. Pittinsky. *Working Fathers: New Strategies for Balancing Work and Family.* Reading, Mass.: Addison-Wesley, 1997.

Lorde, Audre. *Sister Outsider: Essays and Speeches by Audre Lorde.* Freedom, Calif.: Crossing Press, 1984.

Luker, Kristin. *Dubious Conceptions: The Politics of Teenage Pregnancy.* Cambridge: Harvard University Press, 1996.

Macdonald, Cameron Lynne, and Carmen Sirianni, eds. *Working in the Service Society.* Philadelphia, Penn.: Temple University Press, 1996.

Marable, Manning. *Blackwater: Historical Studies in Race, Class Consciousness, and Revolution.* Niwot, Colo.: University Press of Colorado, 1981; rev. ed. 1993.

Martin, Joan. *More Than Chains and Toil: A Christian Work Ethic of Enslaved Women.* Louisville, Ky.: Westminster John Knox Press, 2000.

Mason, Mary Ann, Arlene Skolnick, and Stephen D. Sugarman, eds. *All Our Families: New Policies for a New Century.* New York: Oxford University Press, 1998.

Matthaei, Julie. *An Economic History of Women in America: Women's Work, the Sexual Division of Labor, and the Development of Capitalism.* New York: Schocker Books, 1982.

McCloskey, Donald. *If You're So Smart: The Narrative of Economic Expertise.* Chicago: University of Chicago Press, 1990.

McLanahan, Sara, and Gary Sandefur. *Growing Up with a Single Parent: What Helps, What Hurts.* Cambridge: Harvard University Press, 1994.

Meeks, M. Douglas. *God the Economist: The Doctrine of God and Political Economy.* Minneapolis: Fortress Press, 1989.

Michigan Assemblies Project. *Welfare Reform: How Families Are Faring in Michigan's Local Communities.* Detroit: Groundwork for a Just World, 1998.

Mink, Gwendolyn. *Welfare's End.* Ithaca, N.Y.: Cornell University Press, 1998.

Mintz, Steven, and Susan Kellogg. *Domestic Revolutions: A Social History of American Family Life.* New York: Free Press, 1988.

Mishel, Lawrence, Jared Bernstein, and John Schmitt. *The State of Working America 1998-1999.* Ithaca, N.Y.: Cornell University Press, 1999.

———. *The State of Working America 2000–2001.* Ithaca, N.Y.: Cornell University Press, 2001.

Mount, Eric, Jr. *Covenant, Community, and the Common Good: An Interpretation of Christian Ethics.* Cleveland: Pilgrim Press, 1999.

Mutari, Ellen, Heather Boushey, and William Fraher IV. *Gender and Political Economy: Incorporating Diversity into Theory and Policy.* Armonk, N.Y.: M.E. Sharpe, 1997.

Nelson, Margaret K., and Joan Smith. *Working Hard and Making Do: Surviving in Small Town America.* Berkeley: University of California Press, 1999.

Novak, Michael. *The Spirit of Democratic Capitalism.* Lanham, Md.: Madison Books, 1982, 1991.

———. *This Hemisphere of Liberty: A Philosophy of the Americas.* Washington, D.C.: American Enterprise Institute, 1992.

O'Connell, Helen. *Women and the Family.* London: Zed Books, 1994.

Okin, Susan Moller. *Justice, Gender, and the Family.* New York: Basic Books, 1989.

Oliver, Melvin L., and Thomas M. Shapiro. *Black Wealth/White Wealth: A New Perspective on Racial Inequality.* New York: Routledge, 1995.

Paleczny, Barbara. *Clothed In Integrity: Weaving Just Cultural Relations and the Garment Industry.* Waterloo, Ontario: Wilfrid Laurier University Press, 2000.

Parasuraman, Saroj, and Jeffrey H. Greenhaus, eds. *Integrating Work and Family: Challenges and Choices for a Changing World.* Westport, Conn.: Quorum Books, 1997.

Rasmussen, Larry. *Earth Community Earth Ethics.* Maryknoll, N.Y.: Orbis, 1996.

———. *Moral Fragments and Moral Community: A Proposal for Church in Society.* Minneapolis: Fortress Press, 1993.

Reiter, Reyna, ed. *Toward an Anthropology of Women.* New York: Monthly Review Press, 1975.

Robb, Carol S. *Equal: An Ethical Approach to Economics and Sex.* Boston: Beacon Press, 1995.

Ruether, Rosemary Radford. *Sexism and God-Talk: Toward a Feminist Theology.* Boston: Beacon Press, 1983.

———. *Christianity and the Making of the Modern Family*. Boston: Beacon Press, 2000.

Schein, Virginia E. *Working from the Margins: Voices of Mothers in Poverty*. Ithaca, N.Y.: Cornell University Press, 1995.

Schor, Juliet. *The Overworked American: The Unexpected Decline of Leisure*. New York: Basic Books, 1991.

Schwartz, Pepper. *Love Between Equals: How Peer Marriage Really Works*. New York: Free Press, 1995.

Sennett, Richard. *The Corrosion of Character: The Personal Consequences of Work in the New Capitalism*. New York: W. W. Norton, 1998.

Shaw, Stephanie J. *What a Woman Ought to Be and to Do: Black Professional Women Workers During the Jim Crow Era*. Chicago: University of Chicago Press, 1996.

Smith-Rosenberg, Carroll. *Disorderly Conduct: Visions of Gender in Victorian America*. New York: Alfred A. Knopf, 1985.

Stackhouse, Max L. *Public Theology and Political Economy: Christian Stewardship in Modern Society*. Grand Rapids, Mich.: Wm. B. Eerdmans, 1987.

———, Peter L. Berger, Dennis P. McCann, and M. Douglas Meeks. *Christian Social Ethics in a Global Era*. Nashville: Abingdon Press, 1995.

———, with Peter J. Paris, eds. *God and Globalization*, Vol. 1, *Religion and the Powers of the Common Life*. Harrisburg, Penn.: Trinity Press International, 2000.

———, with Don S. Browning, eds. *God and Globalization*, Vol. 2, *The Spirit and the Modern Authorities*. Harrisburg, Penn.: Trinity Press International, 2001.

Stacey, Judith. *Brave New Families: Stories of Domestic Upheaval in Late Twentieth Century America*. New York: Basic Books, 1990.

Tilly, Chris. *Short Hours, Short Shrift: Causes and Consequences of Part-Time Work*. Washington, D.C.: Economic Policy Institute, 1990.

Trimiew, Darryl M. *God Bless the Child That's Got Its Own: The Economic Rights Debate*. Atlanta: Scholars Press, 1997.

United States Catholic Bishops. "Economic Justice for All: Catholic Social Teaching and the U.S. Economy," *Origins* 16, no. 24 (27 November 1986).

U.S. Department of Labor, Women's Bureau. *Women Workers: Trends and Issues*. Washington, D.C.: Department of Labor, 1994.

Valian, Virginia. *Why So Slow? The Advancement of Women*. Cambridge, Mass.: MIT Press, 1998.

Wolff, Edward N. *Top Heavy: The Increasing Inequality of Wealth in America and What Can Be Done about It*. New York: New Press, 1996.

Young, Iris Marion. *Justice and the Politics of Difference*. Princeton, N.J.: Princeton University Press, 1990.

Zinn, Howard. *A People's History of the United States, 1492–Present*. Rev. ed. New York: Harper Perennial, 1995.

Zweig, Michael, ed. *Religion and Economic Justice*. Philadelphia: Temple University Press, 1991.

JOURNALS CONSULTED

American Journal of Economics and Sociology
Annual of the Society of Christian Ethics
Family Relations
Gender and Society
Harvard Business Review
Journal of Divorce and Remarriage
Journal of Economic Issues
Journal of Family and Economic Issues
Journal of Marriage and Family
Journal of Poverty
Journal of Religious Ethics
Monthly Labor Review
National Institute Economic Review
Poverty and Race
Theological Studies
Work, Employment and Society

Index